D0598288

MODERN WORLD NATIONS

AFGHANISTAN	IRAN
ARGENTINA	IRAQ
AUSTRALIA	IRELAND
AUSTRIA	ISRAEL
BAHRAIN	ITALY
BERMUDA	JAPAN
BOLIVIA	KAZAKHSTAN
BRAZIL	KENYA
CANADA	KUWAIT
CHINA	MEXICO
COSTA RICA	THE NETHERLANDS
CROATIA	NEW ZEALAND
CUBA	NIGERIA
EGYPT	NORTH KOREA
ENGLAND	NORWAY
ETHIOPIA	PAKISTAN
FRANCE	PERU
REPUBLIC OF GEORGIA	RUSSIA
GERMANY	SAUDI ARABIA
GHANA	SCOTLAND
GUATEMALA	SOUTH AFRICA
ICELAND	SOUTH KOREA
INDIA	UKRAINE

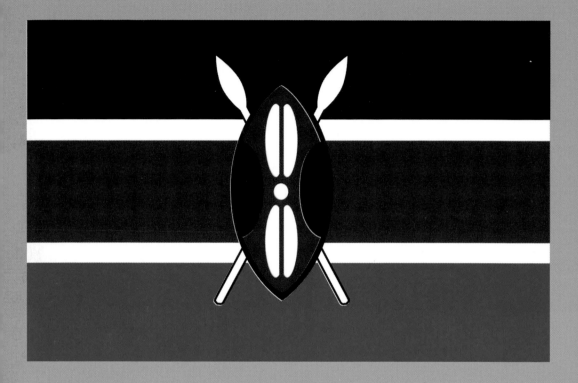

Kenya

Joseph R. Oppong
University of North Texas

and

Esther D. Oppong

Series Consulting Editor
Charles F. Gritzner
South Dakota State University

CHELSEA HOUSE
PUBLISHERS
A Haights Cross Communications Company

Philadelphia

Frontispiece: Flag of Kenya

Cover: Mt. Kilimanjaro seen from Kenya.

CHELSEA HOUSE PUBLISHERS

VP, NEW PRODUCT DEVELOPMENT Sally Cheney
DIRECTOR OF PRODUCTION Kim Shinners
CREATIVE MANAGER Takeshi Takahashi
MANUFACTURING MANAGER Diann Grasse

Staff for KENYA

EXECUTIVE EDITOR Lee Marcott
PRODUCTION ASSISTANT Megan Emery
PICTURE RESEARCHER 21st Century Publishing and Communications, Inc.
SERIES DESIGNER Takeshi Takahashi
COVER DESIGNER Keith Trego
LAYOUT 21st Century Publishing and Communications, Inc.

A Haights Cross Communications Company

http://www.chelseahouse.com

First Printing

1 3 5 7 9 8 6 4 2

Library of Congress Cataloging-in-Publication Data

Oppong, Joseph R.
   Kenya/by Joseph R. Oppong and Esther D. Oppong.
      p. cm.—(Modern world nations)
Includes index.
Summary: Describes the history, geography, government, economy, people, and culture
of Kenya.
   ISBN 0-7910-7474-9
   1. Kenya—Juvenile literature. [1. Kenya.] I. Oppong, Esther D. II. Title. III. Series.
DT433.522.O67 2003
967.62—dc21

                                                                          2003011606

Table of Contents

Kenya

Giraffes amble on the Serengheti Plain in Kenya. The country's wild animals are one of its greatest resources.

1

Introduction

*J*ambo! Welcome to Kenya, the heart of African safari country. Kenya boasts the most diverse collection of wild animals on the continent, and no matter how many Tarzan movies you've seen, nothing will prepare you for the real thing! Kenya has the world's most magnificent wildlife parks. It also has vast stretches of unspoiled beaches, thriving coral reefs, lofty mountains, and ancient Swahili cities.

With an area of about 224,000 square miles (580,000 square kilometers), Kenya is almost as large as the state of Texas. Although it is not the largest or the most populous country in East Africa, it dominates the region. For example, Nairobi is the largest city in East Africa. This modern capital city has towering skyscrapers and its seaport, Mombasa, is the region's busiest.

Perhaps you have heard about Nairobi before, or Mombasa? It was there that the American embassy was bombed in 1998. The bombing, which was blamed on Osama bin Laden's Al Qaeda organization, killed 12 Americans and more than 200 Kenyans. You also may remember hearing about a Mombasa hotel bombing on November 28, 2002. At 8:30 that morning, a car bomb exploded at the Israeli-owned Paradise Hotel, killing 16 people. Three were Israeli tourists (the real targets), three were the bombers, and ten were Kenyans innocently caught in the middle. Osama bin Laden's Al Qaeda claimed responsibility for that too. Although not the targets, Kenyans suffer the worst devastation from both of these attacks.

Tourists! Bombs! American Embassy! Why in Kenya? It is matters such as these that this book is about. This book is also about the geography of Kenya.

Geographers study *where* things are, *why* they are there, and *how* they are important to us. Geographers study anything on Earth's surface. For example, they are interested in physical land features, such as volcanoes, mountains, and valleys. They also study vegetation types such as deserts, rain forests, and prairie grasslands. Climates are of particular interest to geographers as they note whether places are hot or cold, wet or dry, stormy or calm. Geographers try to explain why each of these physical features or conditions is found in different places on Earth's surface and how they are important to people. This is called "physical geography."

But physical features are not the only things that geographers study. They also are interested in humans and what they do and create. The nature and layout of cities, towns, and rural settlements are important. So are cultural practices such as food habits, systems of political organization, and social practices. Even farming methods vary from one place to another. Such variations usually reflect the culture (way of life), including technology, and the different ways people adapt to the natural environment. Geographers try to explain why cultural practices differ from place to place. This is called "human geography."

Kenya provides a wonderfully spectacular setting in which to study both physical and human geography. It boasts snowcapped mountains right on the equator! Spectacular herds of wildlife roam across the country's vast prairie and savanna grasslands! Kenya may be the "cradle of humanity," because some of the earliest evidence of human existence has been discovered in its Great Rift Valley! The country is also full of tourists.

Kenya is snugly tucked away in Eastern Africa. The equator divides the country into two nearly equal parts. It is bordered by five countries and two important water bodies. To the east are Somalia and the Indian Ocean. To the south lies Tanzania. In the west, it borders huge Lake Victoria and Uganda. In the north, Kenya shares a border with Sudan and Ethiopia. Because of its tropical location, you might expect the country to be hot and wet, perhaps covered by dense tropical forests. You may be surprised to find, however, that weather here varies from steaming tropics to parched desert areas. And atop majestic Mount Kenya, snow remains throughout the year even though the peak is located nearly on the equator!

Kenya's physical geography is marvelously diverse. It offers large areas of good farmland that support productive agriculture, scattered pasturelands, and lots of scrub and forest woodlands. Much of northeastern Kenya is a flat, bush-covered plain. The remainder of the country includes immaculate beaches, scenic highlands and lake regions, the Great Rift Valley, and the magnificent Mount Kenya. This is just the beginning of Kenya's appeal. As for natural resources, gold, limestone, soda ash, salt barites, rubies,

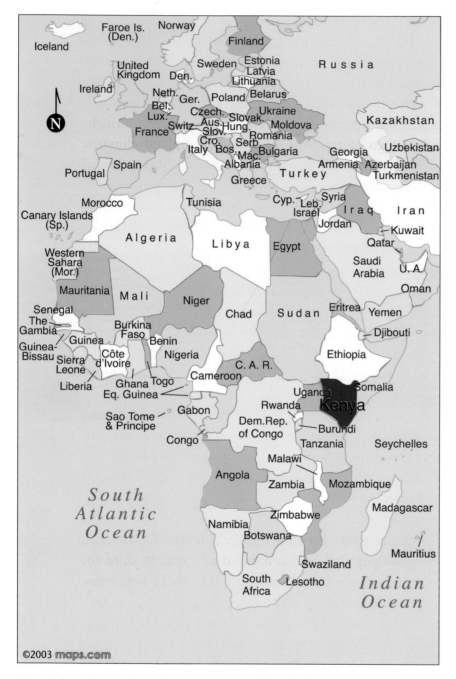

Kenya's location on the Indian Ocean, part of its physical geography, has had a big impact on its human geography.

fluorspar, garnets, wildlife, and hydropower are available in this exciting East African wonderland.

Politically, Kenya was called British East Africa until it gained independence in December of 1963. The richest and most populous of the East African colonies, it was also the last to achieve independence. Whites (European, largely British) hated to let go of this land of temperate upland climates, abundant rich and fertile soils, and astonishing physical beauty. Of course, you also have to consider competition between rival independence movements.

After independence, the country became the "Republic of Kenya," or Kenya, as it is more commonly known. The name comes from its most famous physical feature, Mount Kenya. From independence in 1963, until December 2002, Kenya was ruled by one political party, the Kenya African National Union (KANU), and had only two presidents—Jomo Kenyatta, who ruled from independence until his death in 1978, and Daniel arap Moi. In December 2002, after 24 years in power, the Moi and KANU era ended. Kenya entered a new era with Mwai Kibaki and the National Rainbow Coalition (NARC). From the depressing hopelessness and pessimism that characterized the latter part of the Moi regime, many Kenyans are filled with a new hopeful optimism for a bright future.

Kenya's population is estimated to be just over 31 million. Its people are overwhelmingly (97%) of African descent, although the population is composed of some 40 different ethnic groups. English and Swahili are the official languages, but many indigenous (native) languages also are spoken. Kenya's ethnic diversity has produced a vibrant culture, but is also a source of conflict.

Most Kenyans are subsistence farmers, producing food for their families with little left over for sale to others. This is quite different from commercial agriculture in which farmers produce crops mainly for sale. Tea and coffee are grown for export on much larger landholdings. The economy depends heavily on these agricultural crops and tourism.

Kenya is the primary destination for adventure travel in Africa. It is perhaps the world's finest—and undoubt-edly most famous—safari destination. Safari, however, is by no means the only reason to visit Kenya, for the attractions of its rich culture and diverse environments are considerable.

Unfortunately, petty crime is a major concern in Kenya's urban centers. Nairobi isn't referred to as "Nairobbery" for nothing. Some parts of the city are particularly notorious for muggings. Mombasa's magnificent beaches are also tainted by crime. And sadly, corruption is widespread, nationwide as it is in many of the world's poorer countries.

Kenya has a major problem with the human immuno-deficiency virus that causes Acquired Immune Deficiency Syndrome (HIV-AIDS). In December 2002, 15% of the population between ages 15 and 49 was estimated to be HIV-positive. Nairobi and Mombasa, the major urban centers, are the most affected. The country's health care is in shambles. Once one of Africa's most prosperous and stable countries, Kenya slid into poverty and disrepair under Moi, whose rule was underpinned largely by corruption and patronage politics. More than half of Nairobi's residents live in tin-roofed slums with no running water or electricity. Garbage and human waste collect in piles that children play on because they have no parks or fields in their neighborhoods.

Let us explore this incredibly beautiful, and yet in some ways troubled, country called Kenya. It has East Africa's largest economy, pleasant and sunny California-like weather, and hillsides of mango and banana trees. Plentiful wildlife such as zebras and hippos make it a favorite African safari destination for Americans and Europeans. Are you ready to begin your Kenyan adventure? Then let's go. *Habari!* (Swahili for "Hello!").

Cape buffalo graze on the grasslands of Kenya near Mount Kilimanjaro.

2

A Land of Physical Diversity

K enya's physical geography varies greatly and presents many surprising paradoxes. Majestic snow and glacier-crested volcanic mountains rise right along the equator. Prairie grassland plains, home to a wonderfully diverse collection of wildlife, lie adjacent to rugged terrain and spectacular rift (trench) valleys. Hot springs and tropical forests exist, yet much of the country suffers from persistent drought. Although much of northeastern Kenya is a flat, bush-covered plain, the remainder of the country includes beautiful beaches, scenic highland and lake regions, the Great Rift Valley, and the magnificent Mount Kenya. Let us begin our tour of Kenya's physical geography with a look at its beautiful and varied terrain.

LAND FEATURES

Kenya's 224,000 square mile (580,000 square-kilometer) area is comprised of 218,928 square miles (567,021 square kilometers) of land and 5,200 square miles (13,468 square kilometers) of water. In the south, elevation begins at sea level along the shoreline of the Indian Ocean coastal plain. Moving inland, the land rises in a series of mountain ridges and plateaus that eventually reach an average elevation of about 10,000 feet (3,000 meters) above sea level. A gigantic trench, East Africa's spectacular, steep-sided Great Rift Valley cuts a 30- to 40-mile-wide swath through this plateau just north of Nairobi. The highest terrain is in the center of the country. Here, snowcapped Mount Kenya rises to an elevation of 17,058 feet (5,199 meters). In Africa, only Mount Kilimanjaro, which towers 19,340 feet (5,895 meters) over neighboring Tanzania, is higher. Much of the south and southwest is covered with scattered mountains and plains, before descending to the shores of Lake Victoria in the west.

The Great Rift Valley and central highlands form the country's backbone. This region also is where Kenya offers its most spectacular scenery. The Great Rift Valley, a great gash in the Earth's crust, cuts across the country. East of the rift, the central highlands slope down to grassy plains, dry thorn bush country, and the ocean. The humid coastal belt includes the Tana River estuary and a string of good beaches. Western Kenya takes in the fertile fringes of Lake Victoria and is home to some prime game parks. The vast, arid northeastern region is where Kenya is at its wildest and most untouched by the modern world.

WEATHER AND CLIMATE

Kenya's weather (daily conditions) and climate (long-term average weather) are as varied as its terrain. Both are influenced by two primary factors: the country's equatorial location and variations in elevation. The country's tropical location means that daily and seasonal temperature variations are not as great as they are in the middle latitudes. Elevation, however, is the most important factor determining temperature differences across the country.

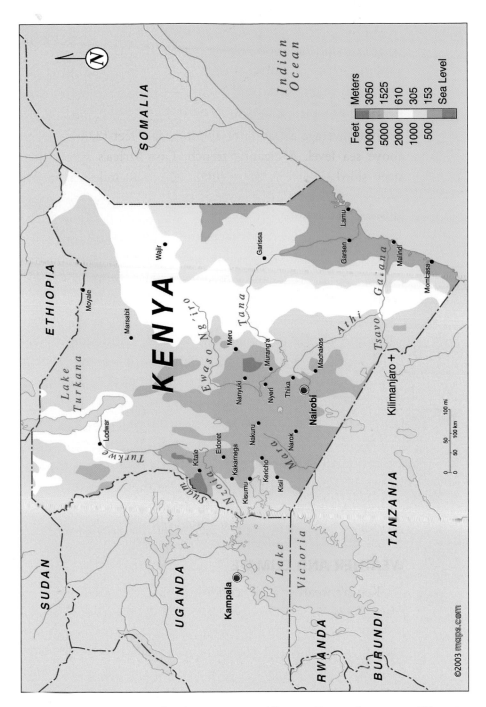

Kenya's 224,000 square miles (580,160 square kilometers) experience very different temperatures and climates that change by location and climate.

Climatic conditions vary from the steaming humid tropical conditions of the coastal region, to the dry desert heat of the eastern interior and northern plains, to the cool to cold conditions of the high plateau and mountain regions. Along the ocean coast, conditions are extremely humid and daily temperatures average 80°F (27°C). Moving inland and upward in elevation, temperatures decrease by about 3°F (2°C) with each 1,000-foot (305-meter) increase in elevation. This explains why, despite Kenya's equatorial position, Mount Kenya is perpetually snowcapped. Similarly, Nairobi, at an elevation of 5,500 feet (1,670 meters), has an average annual temperature of a very pleasant 67°F (19°C). The highlands generally have a cool, spring-like climate with a mean annual maximum of 79°F (26.1°C) and a mean annual minimum of 50°F (10°C).

Kenya's highest temperatures are found in the northern plain, where the average maximum is 93°F (34°C) and temperatures often reach 110°F (43.3°C). This reflects still another climate control factor, the geographic principle of continentality. Areas that are distant from large water bodies have greater variations in temperature than lands close to water. In the same way, areas that are near to large water bodies have milder temperatures and lower annual variations in temperature. Throughout most of Kenya, temperatures are comfortably warm year-round.

Much of Kenya experiences heavy rainfall from March through May and, to a lesser extent, from October through December. The best time for most outdoor activities (including safari and mountain climbing) is during the dry season that extends from June into September. Location is a key factor in determining the amount and distribution of precipitation (falling moisture in any form) in Kenya. In the western plateau and highlands, rain falls in a single long season. East of the Great Rift Valley, there are two distinct seasons: a long period of rains from March to May and a shorter season from September to October. Rainfall is most plentiful in the highlands and on the coast, both of which receive an annual average of 40 to 60 inches

(100–150 centimeters). The western plateau receives over 70 inches (180 centimeters) of moisture annually. More than 70% of the country, however, is arid or semiarid, receiving less than 20 inches (50 centimeters) per year. Rainfall is sporadic in the dry areas.

WATER FEATURES

Kenya is fortunate to have a number of water features, including ocean, lakes, rivers, and their associated environments. The Indian Ocean washes the shores of Kenya's 334-mile (536-kilometer) long coastal plain. In addition, Kenya shares the vast waters of Africa's largest freshwater body, Lake Victoria, with its western neighbors—Tanzania and Uganda.

The country's principal drainage system begins in the interior highlands. From this elevated region, streams and rivers flow eastward toward the Indian Ocean, westward to Lake Victoria, and northward to Lake Rudolf. Some northward flowing streams simply disappear in the desert terrain of northern Kenya. A secondary drainage system is formed by rivers in the southern highlands of Ethiopia, which extend into Kenya along the eastern part of their shared boundary. These rivers are seasonal. Those receiving sufficient rainwater to reach the sea all pass through Somalia.

Kenya's two largest and only navigable rivers are the Tana and the Galana, both of which flow into the Indian Ocean. The Tana basin has an area of about 24,000 square miles (62,160 square kilometers) and receives much of the flow from the Aberdare Range and Mount Kenya. The Galana River has its source in the southeastern Kenya highlands and flows together with its tributaries into the Indian Ocean north of Malindi.

Kenya's western highlands are drained by a number of rivers that empty into Lake Victoria. Two of the streams, the Nzoia and Yala, have waterfalls that offer considerable potential for generating hydroelectric power. The Mara River, in the Mau escarpment in the southwest highlands, flows southward for about 100 miles (160 kilometers), enters Tanzania, and turns westward to eventually reach Lake Victoria. East of the Great Rift Valley, small streams flowing from the northern Kenya highlands either disappear in the arid land, or reach the Indian Ocean with their meager flow.

PLANT AND ANIMAL LIFE

Kenya's flora (plants) and fauna (animals) offer an incredible diversity of species, size, and appearance. The vast plains of the south are dotted with flat-topped acacia trees, thorn bushes, and the distinctive bottle-shaped baobab tree. On the slopes of Mount Elgon and Mount Kenya, bamboo forests thrive. Further upslope can be found the bizarre groundsel tree, with its huge cabbage-like flowers, and giant lobelias with long spikes. Completing the diversity are mangrove forests and coconut palms on the coast, savannah grass and woodlands, and thick coniferous evergreen forests on the mountain slopes. On the western plateaus, scattered low trees grow amid savanna grasses over five feet (1.5 meters) tall. Similar vegetation is found on the plateaus east and south of Mount Kenya. On the northern and southern edges of the highlands, flat-topped acacia trees are scattered about the savanna (tall grass) landscape.

Kenya's parks and reserves are home to many birds and animals. There are over 1,000 species of birds, including flamingos and lovebirds. Some of the animals that can be found in the reserves include lions, cheetahs, and leopards. There are elephants, giraffes, zebras, and rhinos, as well as many smaller grazing animals. And waters teem with crocodiles, fish, and the occasional hippopotamus. As you travel Kenya, not only can you visit different environments, but you certainly will find a great variety of wildlife to greet you wherever you go!

ENVIRONMENTAL PROBLEMS

A number of environmental concerns plague Kenya and its people. They include problems related to water, deforestation, soil erosion, desertification, and poaching of wildlife. Water is one of the chief problems. The north and east suffer frequent and often severe droughts. Crops and grasslands wither, streams dry up, and livestock and wildlife suffer. Here and elsewhere, during the rainy season, massive flooding can occur. In addition, water pollution from urban and industrial wastes is a problem in cities, just as a loss of water quality from increased use of pesticides and fertilizers poses problems in many rural areas.

A growing human population increasingly threatens Kenya's wildlife habitats. Many farmers, struggling to raise enough food just to survive, are being forced onto marginal land that is unsuitable for agriculture and traditional animal rearing. As a result, many lands surrounding protected areas are being converted to food production using methods hostile to most wildlife. Additionally, Kenya's previously nomadic peoples, such as the Maasai and their cattle herds, have been confined to increasingly smaller plots of land. As their population has expanded, overgrazing of livestock has resulted in the devastation of rangeland. Having coexisted for centuries, the herders now see wildlife as competitors for scarce water and grazing resources. Legal and illegal hunting (poaching) is also sharply reducing wildlife populations. Loss of habitat and widespread poaching are taking their toll on Kenya's irreplaceable wildlife. It is feared that as wildlife disappears, so will the vital tourism that it supports.

Kenya's forests also are disappearing at an alarming rate. When forests are removed, underground water reserves or watersheds become less effective. Water runs off slopes more rapidly, thereby increasing soil erosion. The loss of soil, in turn, poses a serious threat to food production and security and sustained agricultural development. Wetlands also are being drained and cultivated and coastal ecosystems are similarly threatened.

Many environmental concerns also beset Africa's largest freshwater body, Lake Victoria. Problems include deterioration of water quality, loss of biodiversity, and infestation by the water hyacinth—a plant with an attractive bloom, but a dreadful pest that mats the lake's surface. One of Africa's highest densities of population can be found surrounding Lake Victoria. As a result, deforestation, severe soil erosion, wetlands destruction, and loss of water quality combine with huge numbers of people to cause considerable poverty within lake basin communities.

Before we leave the physical geography of Kenya, we must visit one of the world's greatest natural wonders—the Great Rift Valley. This is especially important, because if the geologists are right, in the future, Africa east of the Great Rift Valley will be an island! An ocean will separate it from the continent.

THE GREAT RIFT VALLEY

Most Americans have heard about California's San Andreas fault. But with a length of only 780 miles (1,255 kilometers), it is minor compared to East Africa's 4,000-mile (6,400-kilometers) long Great Rift Valley. The Great Rift Valley is absolutely enormous. It is the longest and most spectacular such feature on the Earth's surface. It extends from the Middle Eastern country of Jordan to near Beira, a city on the coast of Mozambique. The valley is actually a long deep depression with steep, wall-like, cliffs that has an average width of 30 to 40 miles (50-65 kilometers). It is like a huge scar across the earth's surface. Along this scar, the earth is patched with inactive volcanoes and a series of long, narrow lakes.

Lakes within the Great Rift Valley

Lake Baringo, the most northern of Kenya's rift valley lakes, is 451 square miles (1168 square kilometers) in size and has a maximum depth of 39 feet (12 meters). This is one of Kenya's most popular locations for bird-watchers, with over 470 species in the area. Some of the most common include flamingos, herons, eagles, great white egrets and a wide variety of hornbills. The lake is home to an abundant variety of fish, hippos, crocodiles and monitor lizards.

The Great Rift Valley is actually a geological fault that developed when the continents first formed millions of years ago. It may signal yet another change in the future topography of Kenya.

Lying just south of Lake Baringo, Bogoria is a long, thin "soda lake" with boiling hot springs and steaming geysers set in rocky outcrops. This is a popular birding spot for seeing flamingos, especially when Lake Nakuru's water level is low. Other wildlife includes the rare greater kudu, and near its shores can be found cheetahs, hyenas, jackals, and leopards.

Lake Nakuru is a shallow alkaline soda lake set beneath the high cliffs of the eastern Great Rift Valley. It is a flamingo paradise offering the spectacular view of up to 2 million flamingos at one time (during the season) along with hundreds of other species including birds of prey. Other wildlife here includes giraffes and black rhinos.

Lake Naivasha in the Great Rift Valley is part of Kenya's water system that supports an abundant plant and animal life.

Lake Turkana (formerly Lake Rudolph) is the largest of Kenya's rift valley lakes and the fourth-largest in all of Africa. It extends southward from the Ethiopian border for a distance of nearly 200 miles (325 kilometers) and reaches a width of 30 miles (48 kilometers) at its widest point. Turkana is fondly called the Jade Sea because of its strikingly beautiful color. It is also the world's largest permanent lake located within a desert environment. The lake has many things to offer, including one of the world's largest crocodile populations, some of which reach massive sizes.

Origin of the Great Rift Valley

What could possibly cause such a feature as Africa's Great Rift Valley? Geologists believe that the continents were originally one huge landmass. Violent forces working from deep beneath the surface began tearing apart the Earth's crust. Through millions of years, today's continents began to form. These forces caused huge chunks of the crust to sink between parallel fault lines. They also forced up molten rock in volcanic eruptions. Ultimately, when these huge depressions filled with huge volumes of water, the breakup was complete. For example, the African continent fits like a jigsaw puzzle piece between North and South America. Spreading processes tore Saudi Arabia away from the rest of the African continent, forming the Red Sea. Similarly, Madagascar was torn away from Africa.

The U.S. Geological Survey (USGS) suggests that a new spreading center may be developing under Africa along the East African Rift Zone. If spreading continues, the three plates that meet at the edge of the present-day African continent will separate completely, allowing the Indian Ocean to flood the area. This will make the easternmost corner of Africa (the Horn of Africa) a large island. Thus, East Africa might be the site of the Earth's next major ocean!

Having now completed our tour of Kenya's striking physical geography, let's turn our attention to its equally incredible past. Before considering the country's long, complex, and fascinating history, it is appropriate to learn a new word: *Karibu* (kah-REE-boo), meaning "Welcome" in Swahili. Karibu to Kenya's past!

These Karo tribespeople could tell you that recent challenges for Kenya are the same for the whole continent: oppressive colonial rule, a hard-won fight for independence, tribal conflict, a struggling economy, and devastating disease.

3

Kenya
Through Time

INTRODUCTION

Have you ever wondered what the physical surroundings of the first humans were like? Perhaps it was a place of pristine forests and grasslands, with vast numbers of animals living harmoniously with our early ancestors in a Garden of Eden setting! Where might such an environment have been located? In Kenya, you are in the immediate area that archaeologists (scientists who study early humans) believe was the earliest homeland of humankind.

Kenya may have a longer history than any other place on Earth. Many famous archaeologists, such as the Leakey family (Louis, his wife Mary, and son Richard), believe what is now southern Kenya may have been the homeland of humankind. From this cradle of humanity, their descendants moved out to populate the world. Wave upon wave of migrants from all over Africa and the

Middle East also passed through the region. Thus, Kenya has probably experienced a human presence since the appearance of the human species more than a million years ago. Some of the oldest human remains have been found around Lake Victoria, in the Kenyan highlands, and in the Great Rift Valley region. Archaeologists suggest that hand axes and cleavers discovered at these sites were probably used as all-purpose tools to cut and skin meat during the early to late Stone Age period.

Much later, the bow and arrow were introduced. In the Late Stone Age (3000–1000 B.C.), there is evidence of the arrival of a new, tall people with narrow heads and prominent noses and chins. Archaeologists think they resembled some of the present-day people of Somalia and Ethiopia. Nomadic tribes from Ethiopia arrived in about 2000 B.C. A second group followed around 1000 B.C., occupying much of central Kenya.

Migration of the Bantu people into East Africa began around 400 A.D. Kenya's remaining people arrived from many different places across the continent between 500 B.C. and 500 A.D. Bantu-speaking people (such as the Gusii, Kikuyu, Akamba, and Meru) arrived from West Africa. Nilotic speakers (Maasai, Luo, Samburu, and Turkana) came from the Nile Valley in southern Sudan.

ARABS AND ISLAM

When people move to a new location, they take their most important things with them, such as household utensils, tools, jewelry, and family mementos. They also take their knowledge, food habits, farming methods, language, and religion; in short, they carry their culture (or way of life), with them. This is one important way culture can spread. Geographers call this *relocation diffusion*. As people *relocate* (move), they *diffuse* (spread) their culture. Thus when Europeans moved to North America, they brought European cultural practices to North America.

Muslims from the Arabian Peninsula and Shirazis from Persia (now Iran) settled along the East African coast. They brought with them their Islamic faith, the Arabic language, dome-shaped architecture, Muslim dress, and other important aspects of their way of life. Thus, the arrival of Arabs marked the beginning of Islam in Kenya. Beginning in about 700 A.D., considerable trade occurred across the Indian Ocean between the Arabs, Phoenicians, Indians, and Chinese. They traded cloth, pottery, and glass beads in exchange for cowry shells, iron products, and mangrove poles. Knowledge of ironworking came to the Bantu (native Africans) around 900 A.D.

Why did so many people arrive in Kenya by sea in ancient times? Before the advent of modern navigation and large, steam-powered, ocean-going vessels, ocean travel was a very risky and tedious business. Prevailing winds were a major factor in the direction and speed of ocean travel. Some areas had the advantage of location, but others did not. Kenya's location made it very accessible to sailors. Seasonal monsoon winds occur along the East African coast from December to March, easing travel by blowing vessels westward toward Kenya's coast. Moreover, Mombasa provided an excellent natural harbor.

PORTUGUESE TRADERS

Drawn by the lure of spices and gold, the Portuguese, led by Vasco da Gama, rounded South Africa's Cape of Good Hope and sailed northward along Africa's eastern coast. Aided by the monsoons, they landed on the Kenyan coast in 1498. By the end of the sixteenth century, they controlled much of the country, including Mombasa. They, too, played a major role in shaping Kenya's culture, just as the Muslim Arabs had previously. Portuguese traders brought Christianity. They also introduced pineapples, bananas, maize, cassava, and even a few words that are now part of the Swahili language.

The Portuguese built a colony along Kenya's coast and established themselves as a dominant power in the area. They used the natural port of Mombasa as their base and set up a port garrison of troops. Between 1500 and 1509, however, the Portuguese faced fierce resistance from the Arabs. Portugal soon sent soldiers with ships and guns to conquer the Arab-Swahili settlements of the east coast. Arabs tried to defend their trading lands, but the Portuguese were stronger. The Portuguese soldiers took everything valuable from the towns and burnt them. Some of the most beautiful buildings were burned to the ground.

Where were the Africans while the Arabs and Portuguese were fighting for their land? In Mombasa, Africans joined their Arab friends in fighting against the Portuguese. Only they shot arrows and threw spears at the enemy, while the Arabs fought with swords and daggers. But the Portuguese soldiers had guns and wore leather and metal armor. They easily defeated the people of Mombasa and took gold, silver, silk, and spices from their houses. Later, Mombasa townspeople attacked the Portuguese whenever they could. Mombasa was called "The Island of the War" because it was always the most difficult town to rule. Houses, other buildings, and even the beautiful rows of coconut palms lining the beach were destroyed several times by the Portuguese.

Unlike the people of Mombasa, the people of Malindi welcomed the Portuguese and remained friendly the entire time the Portuguese were in East Africa. Vasco da Gama established good relations with the ruler or sheikh of the town. Consequently, Malindi became the Portuguese's northern headquarters on the East African coast in 1512. However, in 1593 they moved back to Mombasa. Mombasa had a better location, a much better natural harbor, and the trading was more profitable. To defend against any further Arab attacks, they built Fort Jesus, now an important tourist attraction. From this fort, they could see any approaching ship and easily

Fort Jesus was built by the Portuguese, the first European settlers in Kenya, in the 1590s to protect against attack by Arabs.

attack it with cannons if necessary. The Portuguese were finally expelled from Mombasa in 1729, after being in the region for about 200 years. Two Arab dynasties replaced them—the Busaidi dynasty and the Mazrui dynasty. The Busaidi wrested Mombasa from the Mazrui in 1837. Soon, however, other Europeans would arrive in East Africa.

BRITISH ENTER KENYA

In 1884–1885, a conference was held in Berlin (Germany) during which European powers divided Africa among themselves. There was no input from the African people. The British claimed most of what is present-day Kenya. In 1887, the Imperial British East Africa Company received commercial or concessionary rights to the Kenya coast from the sultan of Zanzibar. Severe financial difficulties soon led to its takeover by the British government, which established the East Africa Protectorate in 1895. They immediately began building a railroad which by 1901 connected the port of Mombasa to Kisumu on Lake Victoria. When completed, the link facilitated trade with the interior and with Uganda.

In 1903, the Europeans began to settle and established themselves as large-scale farmers in Kenya's interior highlands. Land was taken from the Kikuyu, Maasai, and others. At the same time, Indian merchants also moved inland from the coast. In 1920, the territory was renamed and its administration was changed. The interior became Kenya Colony and a coastal strip (10-miles [16-kilometers] wide), centering on Mombasa, became the Protectorate of Kenya. From 1920 to 1940, European settlers controlled the government and owned extensive farmlands. Indians maintained small trade establishments and were middle-level government employees. Africans were the lowest class in Kenyan society. They were subsistence farmers, or worked as laborers in the towns (especially Nairobi).

KENYA'S WHITE HIGHLANDS

In essence, the European settlers took most of the best agricultural land, forcing native peoples into less fertile and less desirable areas. There was little that the Africans could do. They were no match for the Europeans who were armed with much more powerful weapons. For the time, at least, they had to accept their situation.

Europeans were unaccustomed to the hot, steaming, tropical conditions of the coastal lowlands. They preferred to live in the cooler interior highlands, at least 5,000 feet (1,524 meters) above sea level where temperatures were similar to those of their homeland. Laws were passed that reserved the highlands solely for European ownership and use. Non-Europeans could not own or cultivate land in the white highlands. As additional white settlers arrived and demanded more fertile land, the Maasai were forcibly evacuated into smaller, less fertile lands called reserves. The Kikuyu, a Bantu agricultural tribe from the Highlands west of Mount Kenya, also had vast tracts of land taken away from them. This particularly frustrated and angered the Africans and Indians. The Indians were angry because they had also wanted the same land and had been in Kenya longer.

Some of Kenya's most fertile land was in the white highlands. The Mombasa-Uganda railway also served the area. Excluding forest reserves, some 12,000 square miles (31,080 square kilometers) of some of the best farmland was included in the white highlands. For example, west of Kisumu the volcanic slopes had weathered to produce a deep, rich, red soil. Ample rains made this some of the country's most productive land. Of course this land was held exclusively by *mzungu* (whites), not Africans or Indians.

Because of these physical advantages, the white highlands became the major contributor to Kenya's economy. Today, the region remains the heart of the country's economy and is the area best served by roads and railways. Flourishing cities include Nairobi, Nakuru, Eldoret, Kitale, Thika, Kericho, and Nyeri. It is also the core of Kenya's industrial activity. Although it covers only 5% of the country's land area, the white highlands produce most of Kenya's agricultural exports, particularly the four leading commodities—coffee, tea, sisal, and pyrethrum.

With the fertile highland area reserved for *mzungu*, most Africans had little or no land. Such land that the natives did have was usually poor and infertile. Under this arrangement, white settlers became increasingly wealthy while Africans remained poor, and the British government protected the white settlers and their lands. With British army support, white settlers were almost invincible. In fact, the Masters and Servants Ordinance of 1906 categorized all white people as masters and all black people as their servants. Koigi wa Wamwere, born in 1949, who saw white rule in Kenya firsthand, wrote:

> Whenever I saw a white man, he carried a gun for killing. Whenever I saw a white man, he wore shoes and socks and made us walk barefoot or wear tire sandals. Whenever I saw a white man, he owned land and we had none. Whenever I saw a white man, he lived in a big house and we in poor huts.

AFRICANS FIGHT BACK

With the white highlands under white control, native peoples became increasingly restless. For obvious reasons, they felt oppressed and could no longer accept such an unfair arrangement. One native tribal group, the Kikuyu, formed an organization — Kikuyu Central Association (KCA) — to oppose European domination. They sent some of their leaders, including Harry Thuku and Jomo Kenyatta, to Europe to ask the British government to remove the injustices and ensure some fairness.

It was not only in land ownership that the Africans were treated unfairly. Other development resources were not fairly distributed either. For example, the colonial government spent 16 times as much educating each white child as it did on each African youngster. Thus, the quality of African education was very poor.

The Mau Mau conflict of the 1920s resulted when native Kenyans rebelled against an unfair colonial government and its treatment of them.

To oppose this exploitation, many other African organizations emerged, usually along tribal lines. The Kenyan Africa Union was formed to create a united front of all tribes in resisting white domination. The terrible Mau Mau struggle was about to begin.

THE MAU MAU CONFLICT

In the 1920s, Africans began to protest their inferior status. Dissent reached a peak between 1952 and 1956 with emergence of the Mau Mau, a complex armed revolt. Led by the Kikuyu, the uprising was a revolt against British rule and a movement to take back traditional land that had been "stolen" by the settlers. Above all, the Mau Mau wanted to end colonial domination and govern themselves. Several events led to the outbreak of violence.

First, during World Wars I and II, many Kenyans fought alongside the British and thousands died. After the wars, those soldiers who survived had been amazingly transformed. While serving in war, these soldiers saw mzungu do work that, in Kenya, only Africans did. They saw mzungu killed and wounded. They learned that, as James Beauttah, one of the African soldiers said, "dirty white men stink just as badly as dirty black men." After the war, the invincibility of mzungu was broken. Mzungu were human and frail, just like the African. These soldiers returned with a confidence and fierce resolve to change the system of mzungu superiority in Kenya.

Second, the colonial government failed to fulfill its promise of providing land and other benefits to ex-servicemen. Instead, their taxes were increased. In a list of grievances sent to the British colonial secretary, Harry Thuku, acting for one of the African organizations, wrote:

> When we went to do war work we were told by His Excellency the governor that we should be rewarded, but it is our reward to have our tax raised and to have registration papers given to us for our ownership of land to be called into question; to be told today that we are to receive title deeds and tomorrow for it to appear that we are not to receive them.

From the end of the Second World War in 1945, the Africans regularly presented their complaints to the colonial government in Nairobi and the British government in London. Under the leadership of Jomo Kenyatta, the Kenyan African Union (KAU) had become a national party with wide support. It also played an important part in demanding a settlement of African grievances. The government, however, did nothing except make promises. Meanwhile the white settlers were themselves pressing Britain for independence under white minority rule. Many Africans began to believe that violence was the only way their goals could be achieved.

In 1946, a Kikuyu group called Anake a Forty (the warriors of 1940) stated that the lost lands could be salvaged only through war. They urged Kenyans to fight for their rights. Members of the Kikuyu, Embu, Meru, and Kamba communities began to swear on oath that they were ready to fight and die for their rights. Here is an example of one of the many oaths:

> I speak the truth and swear before Ngai [God] and before everyone present here that if I am called upon to fight or to kill the enemy, I shall go, even if that enemy be my father or mother, my brother or sister. And if I fail to do this, may this oath kill me, may this thenge [he-goat] kill me, may this seven kill me, may this meat kill me.

The African groups employed such oaths widely to prepare their people for the mass action they considered necessary. The oath always included a commitment to fight for the land that had been seized by Europeans. In fact, Jomo Kenyatta, himself took the oath in 1946. He encouraged the spreading of the oath widely across Kenya.

Meanwhile the British did nothing to persuade Kenyans that reforms would soon be made. In 1947, police opened fire on striking workers at Uplands Bacon Factory, which saw three Africans killed. In 1951, a KAU delegation went to London to present African claims to the colonial secretary, but their demands were rejected. These events infuriated the Africans even more, and they began to openly reject British rule. This meant that Africans who supported the British colonial government or worked for it were seen as enemies and traitors.

In October 1952, the Mau Mau killed Senior Chief Waruhiu, a well-known supporter of the British, in broad daylight. The new governor of Kenya, Sir Evelyn Baring, reacted to this event and the rapidly escalating unrest by declaring a state of emergency on October 20, 1952. That day, six leading African nationalists and KAU officials, including Jomo Kenyatta and Kung'u Karumba, were arrested. They were charged, convicted, and imprisoned for leading Mau Mau, an organization that had been banned. In 1953, KAU and all other national political parties for Africans were banned. This caused the Mau Mau wars to break out in earnest.

On March 26, 1953, the Mau Mau attacked a police station and seized a large haul of weapons and ammunition. That night, 97 Kikuyu who were loyal to the British colonial government, including an ex-chief and 26 members of his family, were massacred. This shocked the British into action. They sent a senior military commander, General George Erskine, with 11 infantry battalions, and 20,000 police officers who worked with 25,000 Kikuyu loyalists to suppress the Mau Mau fighters.

Most of the fighting took place in the central province, Aberdares, around Mount Kenya, and in Nakuru district. As British troops fought the Mau Mau in the forests, the colonial government took strict measures against civilians. An estimated 30,000 Kikuyu living in Nairobi were expelled and some were detained in concentration camps. Many more were forced to live in "protected" villages.

So fierce was the Mau Mau resistance that, despite the much better arms and equipment of the Royal Army and Air Force, the British did not gain the upper hand against the Mau Mau until 1955. Fighting continued in some areas even after 1955. When it was all over, between 600 and 700 of the security forces, including 63 Europeans, had lost their lives. Among the Africans, however, an estimated 11,000 had been killed.

What did the Mau Mau uprising accomplish? The scale of effort needed to put down the uprising convinced the white settlers that they could never rule the country alone. In 1959, freehold land titles in large numbers were issued to Africans. New farm supports were in place, and a campaign was underway to employ landless people. The growth of the agrarian middle class had started to pick up. The seeds for Kenyan independence had been planted.

JOMO KENYATTA'S ROLE

Jomo Kenyatta was in exile from 1952 to 1959. He had been arrested in 1952, tried for Mau Mau crimes, found guilty, and sentenced to seven years of hard labor. Kenyatta's trial and exile, plus his many years in Europe, kept him away from local squabbles and competition that was rampant among the many different African independence groups.

Two of the most dominant groups were the Kenyan African National Union (KANU) and Kenyan African Democratic Union (KADU). KADU was formed specifically to challenge the "danger of Kikuyu-Luo dictatorship." The pastoral tribes whose land had been seized feared that the Kikuyu-dominated KANU would seize the land for Kikuyus and Luos. Similarly, considerable competition among the African leadership was sometimes very intense. Some of the most active leaders included Tom Mboya, Oginga Odinga, and Jomo Kenyatta.

Because Jomo Kenyatta was in prison during the time of rivalry between African groups fighting for independence, he was seen as a nonaligned, unifying agent. This made him politically attractive to many different African factions. Kenyatta's "returning hero" image also gave him the stature to become the unchallenged candidate to lead the new nation.

INDEPENDENCE

On December 12, 1963, Kenya (including both the colony and the protectorate) became independent. A year later, in 1964, the country became a republic, with Jomo Kenyatta as its

Kenya gained its independence in 1963. Kenya's first prime minister, Jomo Kenyatta, wore colobus (monkey) skins at the opening ceremony proclaiming independence after 68 years of British rule.

president. The first decade of independence was characterized by disputes among ethnic groups (especially between the Kikuyu and the Luo), by economic growth and diversification, and by the end of European predominance. Kenya's problems were just beginning.

Many Europeans (who numbered about 55,000 in 1962) and Asians voluntarily left the country. Boundary disputes with Somalia resulted in sporadic fighting (1963–1968). In 1969, Tom Mboya, a leading government official and a possible successor to Kenyatta, was assassinated. Nature also dealt a severe blow as more than 70% of the country was affected by a severe drought during the early 1970s. Kenyatta's silencing of opponents led to further unrest. Throughout the 1970s, relations with neighboring countries deteriorated as well.

Despite these initial problems Kenya has survived as a politically stable country. In fact, the country's future seems quite bright. In the following chapter, attention will focus on this beautiful country's people and culture (way of life). Next, we meet the Kenyan people and learn about their lives.

A majority of Kenyans, 70–75%, are Christian. Notice that the columns in this cathedral in Embu, Kenya, resemble coconut trees.

4

Kenya's People and Culture

Kenya boasts an incredibly vibrant tapestry of cultures and practices. With well over 40 different ethnic groups— representing a mosaic of different languages, customs, beliefs, and lifestyles—Kenya's cultural diversity is both complex and fascinating. It includes both traditional subsistence farmers, seminomadic cattle herders whose diet is comprised of milk and blood drawn from their cattle, and well-educated city dwellers. In this chapter, you will learn about Kenya's people and their way(s) of life. You will learn about their daily lives, what they eat and drink, what kinds of homes they live in, and how they interact with one another. You also will learn about cultural practices that may be contributing to the spread of AIDS in Kenya. In learning about Kenya's people, no doubt you also will find some surprises. Let us go to the heart of Kenya and meet the people.

A DIVERSE POPULATION

In Kenya, a person's name often provides a clear clue of his or her cultural identity. In fact, by knowing a person's name, you can often determine the geographical region of their birth, their tribal and cultural association, their language, and even some of the circumstances of their birth. For example, a name can indicate whether a person was born in the morning or in the afternoon, or whether their birth was during the rainy season or during a drought. All this you can get simply from a person's name!

Kenya's peoples are mostly native Africans, yet they are very diverse. The seven major ethnic groups include: the Kikuyu (22%), Luya (14%), Luo (13%), Kalenjin (12%), Kamba (11%), Kisii (6%), and Meru (6%). Jomo Kenyatta, Kenya's first president, was Kikuyu; Daniel arap Moi, the second president, was Kalenjin. Mwai Kibabki, the third and current president is Kikuyu. Other African ethnic groups make up the remaining 15% of the population. Non-Africans, mostly Asians, Europeans, or Arabs, comprise about 1% of the population. Western cultural values are becoming more accepted while traditional values are changing. Yet, tribal affiliation continues to be the most important part of a person's individual identity.

LANGUAGE

English and Swahili are the two official languages taught throughout the country, but there are many other tribal languages as well. Swahili is a pidgin language and *lingua franca*. When an interacting group of people speak a number of different languages, they often will create a unique language that incorporates words and grammar from two or more of those languages. Such tongues are called pidgin languages.

When one language becomes widely accepted by the otherwise diverse linguistic groups, it becomes a lingua franca. Such languages are commonly used in trade, by the media, and in communication between and among the diverse groups. Swahili, the lingua franca of Kenya and many other parts of eastern Africa, is formed largely from the Arabic and Bantu languages. It is widely spoken especially outside the urban areas and in remote parts of the country. Another language you may encounter is *Sheng*. Younger Kenyans speak it almost exclusively. A fairly recent development, Sheng is a mixture of Swahili and English along with a fair sprinkling of other languages. Imagine, a country in which there is a relatively new language spoken just by the young!

RELIGION

Christianity is the dominant religion throughout Kenya, accounting for 70–75% of the population. Another estimated 10% of Kenyans are Muslims, followers of the Islamic faith. The major Christian faiths are Protestantism (45%) and Roman Catholicism (33%), while Animists (those practicing native religions) account for 18%. Religion in Kenya follows a very fascinating geographic pattern. As we have already learned, Islam is dominant in the coastal region and in the northeastern part of the country bordering Somalia. Islam was introduced centuries ago by Arabic traders who came by ship to coastal ports, conducting trade with people living along the shores of the Indian Ocean. Much of the rest of the country is predominantly Christian. In the more remote tribal areas, a mixture of Islam, Christianity, and native religions is the norm.

There is no official state religion, although the Moi administration tried to associate itself with Christianity, perhaps in the vain hope of gaining some support from the huge Christian majority. During the Moi regime, television news on Sunday included coverage of a weekly church service attended by the political leaders, including Moi and his ministers. Political opponents of the regime enjoyed this media coverage, particularly when they showed scenes of Moi and his ministers yawning or sleeping during services. Lingering images persist in the minds of many Kenyans of Moi and his associates looking awkward whenever the priests spoke of "a culture of corruption," or other hard truths of the previous administration.

SOCIAL STRUCTURE

Traditional pastoralists, rural farmers, Muslims, and urban residents of Nairobi and other cities all contribute to Kenya's cosmopolitan culture. The country's national motto is *harambee*, meaning "pull together." In that spirit, volunteers in hundreds of communities build schools, clinics, and other facilities each year and collect funds to send students abroad.

The social structure that evolved in Kenya during colonial times emphasized race and class. The dominance of whites over blacks was reinforced through segregation of the races and various ethnic groups. Within each ethnic group, status was determined largely by wealth. Historically, though, Kenyans place great importance on the family and its associated traditional values and responsibilities.

Many of Kenya's rural inhabitants live on small farms. Some live in houses made of mud and wooden poles with thatched roofs, while others live in houses of brick or stone with metal roofs. A small number are nomadic livestock herders, notably some of the Maasai people in the south and the Turkana in the north. Wealthy or middle-class city dwellers typically live in modern houses and apartment buildings. Poor, less fortunate, city dwellers live in shanty-towns or slums such as Kibera in Nairobi, or other inexpensive quarters.

In terms of social activities, Kenya's most popular sport is soccer, and Kenyan long-distance runners have gained worldwide renown. Many Kenyans occupy leisure time with traditional music and dance. The overwhelming majority of the Kenyan people dress in Western-style clothing. Some rural Kenyans, however, continue to wear traditional vibrantly colored or patterned garb, such as the single piece of cloth— often bright red in color—worn by the Maasai.

Kenya's ethnic diversity has produced a variety and richness of cultural forms that reflect African, Asian, and European influences. Visual arts are not highly important in contemporary Kenya, although varieties of wood and clay sculpture are produced for the tourist trade. Distinctive forms of music and dance are associated with each of Kenya's ethnic groups, and traditional music has flourished since independence. Kenya also has a thriving industry in popular music, which combines Western and African influences.

Kinship

A keen sense of kinship has been one of the strongest forces in traditional Kenyan society. Kinship is determined through bloodline and marriage. It controls social relationships, governs marital customs, and determines behavior towards others. In traditional Kenyan society, family structure is basically the same as in the United States. A family may include parents, children, grandparents, uncles and aunts, and brothers and sisters who may have their own children. In Kenya, however, this extended family also includes the dead and those yet to be born. The household is the smallest unit of the family. If a man has two or more wives, which is quite common in Kenya, he will have multiple households. Each wife usually will have her own house erected within the same compound where other wives and their households live.

In Kenyan society, the individual does not exist alone, but is simply part of the whole, the kin group. When one person suffers, the whole kin group shares in the suffering. Similarly, rejoicing and mourning also are shared by the

In Kenya, everyone is part of a kin group that helps out relatives in need. One is never alone or lonely, as you can see from this extended family near Marsabit, Kenya.

entire family group, as well as relatives both living and dead and often neighbors. Marriage is not between two individuals, but between two extended families. Thus, children belong to the corporate body of kinsmen, even if they bear only their father's name. Whatever happens to the individual happens to the whole group, and whatever happens to the whole group happens to the individual. This explains why funerals are such elaborate and expensive ceremonies in Kenya today.

Initiation

Initiation is widespread in traditional Kenyan society, but the form it takes differs from community to community. It usually involves a period during which the young initiate withdraws from home and society to receive secret instructions from people qualified to offer such advice. Such initiation introduces the candidates to adult life. After experiencing this formality, the new initiate is allowed to share in the full privileges and duties of the community.

Dancing and beer drinking normally follow initiation. Boys are circumcised while girls undergo clitoridectomy (female genital mutilation). Male circumcision is still widely practiced today and encouraged as a protection against HIV-AIDS. The equivalent female procedure is less widely practiced today. In fact, there had been a massive global outcry against the practice.

Among the Maasai, the young people who have been initiated together became mystically and ritually bound to each other for the rest of their life. They became one body, one group, one community, and one people. They help one another in all kinds of ways.

MARRIAGE AND FAMILY

Marriage is a complex affair in traditional Kenyan society. It is the point at which all the members of a community meet, including the dead, the living, and those yet to be born. Every person expects to marry and become a parent. In fact, marriage is believed to be the final step in the transition to maturity. To be unmarried represents childhood; to be married represents maturity and is a blessing. Until a baby is born to a newly married couple, however, the marriage is considered incomplete, and can even be dissolved.

So, how are marriage partners selected in Kenya? Could you, for example, marry your high-school sweetheart? That depends on your tribal group. In some Kenyan cultures, the parents and relatives of a young man approach the parents of a particular girl to negotiate marriage. This may be considered an arranged marriage. In other parts of society, the young people themselves discover each other and then inform their parents, who will then begin the formal negotiations. In the latter arrangement, you may, indeed, marry your sweetheart. Both sets of parents must agree, though, and marriage between close relatives is strictly forbidden.

The actual wedding ceremony is an elaborate celebration that lasts for many days and includes many rituals. The groom's family presents a gift to the bride's family. This gift has many names such as "bride wealth," "bride-price," and "dowry." It may be in the form of cattle, money, foodstuffs, or other articles of value. It expresses gratitude to the bride's family for raising her and allowing her to become a wife to the groom. Although it may seem so by western viewers, the practice is not payment to buy the bride.

When the marriage rites are complete, the couple moves into their special house. Virginity until marriage is treasured greatly. A virgin bride is the greatest glory and crown to her parents, husband, and relatives. Pregnancy is considered the final seal of marriage and a sign of integration of the woman into her husband's family and kinship group. The birth of a child is cause for a major extended family celebration.

Polygamy

Polygamy (the practice of having multiple wives) exists among all social classes and ethnic groups in Kenya. It is most common, however, within traditional Kenyan society. A man may have two or more wives, but a woman may have only one husband. Infertility is a common reason for polygamy. If the first wife has no children, or only daughters, her husband is expected to add another wife. This, it is believed, will increase the chances of fertility, thereby removing the shame and stigma of being a childless male. It is also believed that taking one or more additional wives will improve the chances of having a prized male child and heir, specifically.

When a family is made up of several wives with their households, it means that in time of need there is always someone around to help. This practice can be thought of as being a "corporate existence." For example, when one wife gives birth, other wives care for her and her children. If one wife dies, the others take care of her children. In case of sickness, other wives take care of household chores such as fetching water from the river and collecting firewood. Running water and gas and electric stoves, after all, are very rare in rural Kenya. Thus, help with such household necessities during sickness may be very useful. However, polygamy increases the spread of HIV-AIDS and other sexually transmitted diseases. When one wife becomes infected, both the husband and all other wives risk infection. Stories of whole families killed by AIDS are quite widespread in the polygamous societies of Kenya.

Wife Inheritance and AIDS

The custom of inheriting the wife of a deceased brother is fairly common. This guarantees care for the widow and her children. The brother, who inherits the wife and children of his deceased relative, performs all of the duties of a husband and father. The children born after this inheritance generally belong to the deceased man. This has been seen as a source of HIV spread since the widow of a man who died from HIV-AIDS is usually infected and may infect her new husband who in turn infects his other wives.

Millicent Akinyi Dula lives in Asembo Bay, a small fishing community on the shores of Lake Victoria in western Kenya. She is a member of the Luo tribe, which practices polygamy and wife inheritance. A few months ago Millicent's husband died, leaving her with six children. According to Luo custom, Millicent was expected to marry her brother-in-law, regardless of how many wives he already had. This is the traditional Luo way of supporting a widow. But Millicent refused. As a strong Christian she did not believe in polygamy, and with her work as a midwife, she also felt economically independent. So, at her husband's funeral, she stood in front of the coffin and

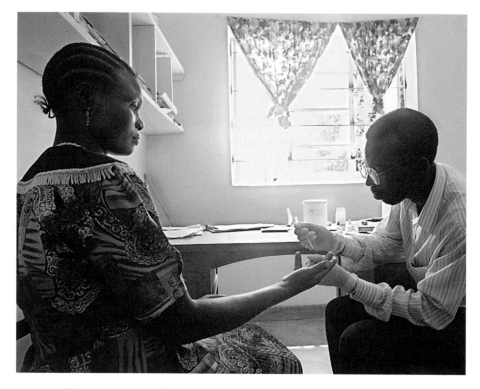

The custom of wife inheritance has helped spread the deadly disease, HIV-AIDS. A widow, whose husband died 2 years ago of AIDS, gets a blood test to check for infection.

informed the mourners that she was going to remain single. It was not an easy announcement to make, many of the people present simply did not believe her. In fact, many people in her community expect her to change her mind. Because of her decision, Millicent has had difficulties in her work. Some women refuse to let her deliver their babies because they believe that a widowed woman who remains single brings death into a house.

Millicent had another very practical reason for refusing to remarry. She does not know exactly what her 44-year-old husband died of, but she is aware of the possibility of AIDS. She has not had herself tested, but she would not want to risk spreading the HIV infection through her brother-in-law's family, or indeed, become infected herself. She has no idea of the sexual history of the man she was expected to sleep with.

Western Kenya has one of the highest rates of HIV infection in the country and wife inheritance is considered a major contributing factor. To limit this spread of the disease, the Luo Council of Elders is now advocating a new concept— that a widow be only symbolically remarried to a brother-in-law. No romantic physical activity is involved, but the community knows that the widow has become part of a new family and her economic needs will be met.

For many young, urban, educated Luo, wife inheritance already belongs to the past. But in the rural areas around Lake Victoria, old customs are hard to change. Informing people about HIV spread is an uphill struggle among the Luo, because many people believe that AIDS is a result of "Chira"—punishment for something done wrong.

Naming

Kenyan children are named in an elaborate ceremony and the names, themselves, are quite unique and revealing. A few days after the birth of a child, relatives and friends are invited for the naming ceremony. Most Kenyans have three names, such as Anne Wairimu Kimani, or John Ndungu Kamau. At home, Anne Wairimu Kimani might call herself Anne Wairimu on some occasions and Anne Kimani on other occasions.

A child's name depends on the nature of its birth and hereditary names such as those of dead relatives or family friends. For example, among the Kamba, a baby girl born at night is named Nduku while a boy is Mutuku. In situations where a child is born after the expected date, it is named Mutua if a boy and Mwikali if a girl. Wambua is the name given to a boy born on a rainy day; but for a girl, it is Syombua. When a woman gives birth on her way to the traditional birth attendant's home, the baby boy is named Mwanzia and a baby girl Nzilani, meaning one born by the roadside. A female child named after a dead relative is named Kasyoka and a male one Musyoka.

In contrast, among the Luo, Ochieng is the name given to a male child born during the afternoon; the female equivalent is called Achieng. Similarly, a boy born early in the morning is called Onyango, but a girl is called Anyango. One of the authors' Kenyan friends is called Tom Ochieng Kidenda. Kidenda is Tom's family name. He inherited this name from his father, who got it from his father. Ochieng describes the circumstances of his birth (male born during the afternoon). Tom is short for Thomas, the name Tom acquired at Christian baptism.

So what would your name be if you were born in Kenya? That is a difficult question. You will have to ask your parents about your birth circumstances!

PARTY TIME, KENYA STYLE

Kenyans love to party! *Benga*, the dominant contemporary dance music, originated among the Luo of western Kenya. Some well-known exponents of benga include Shirati Jazz, Victoria Jazz, and the Ambira Boys. Kenyans love their beer almost as much as they do their dancing. The local brewing industry is thriving.

Nairobi and Mombasa both offer a good selection of dance clubs. Some clubs offer live entertainment. Others feature discos with a disc jockey. Local theaters are located in Nairobi and Mombasa, providing productions of popular plays. Many hotels and lodges provide evening entertainment. Often this will include traditional tribal dancing. This is truly entertaining and an activity not to be missed. The Maasai show their tremendous athletic skills in their dances which feature leaping contests. The dances are accompanied with traditional tribal songs.

FOOD

Did you know that tea is one of Kenya's main exports? In fact, Kenya exports more tea than Sri Lanka, India, and China! *Chai* is Swahili for tea and also is used in reference to a bribe. Teatime in Kenya is a British colonial holdover, but the style of tea is borrowed from India. Chai is tea with milk and sugar. Asian chai also has spices such as cinnamon, cardamom, or ginger in it. Other names for chai are spiced tea, spiced milk tea, milk tea, or even tea latte. Chai is served at breakfast, morning break, after lunch, afternoon tea, after dinner. It is the beverage of choice for most Kenyans.

Indian cuisine has influenced Kenyan food and several Indian classics have become very typical Kenyan dishes. For example, *chapati*, a flat bread, is a very common food on Kenya's dinner tables. *Samosas*, meat-filled fried dumplings, are sold everywhere, from street vendors to fast food restaurants and they make a tasty snack. *Githeri* is a stew made from maize (corn) and beans. It is a hardy, filling dish to which many different vegetables and sometimes meat is added. Goat is a popular meat. When it comes to *nyama choma*, meat roasted over a wood or charcoal fire, though, it is often beef. As with samosas, nyama choma can be found almost anywhere. Kenyan cuisine generally consists of *stodge* filler with beans or a meat sauce. If you had to name a national dish in Kenya, it would probably be nyama choma (barbecued goat meat).

Running and Diet — Is there a Kenyan Secret?

Whatever the event—a road race, track meet, or cross-country run—do not bet against a Kenyan. Kenyan runners are legendary for their unique ability to recover from daily bouts of strenuous training and to perform well when it really counts. Since it is impossible to train hard and race well without optimal nutrition, what role does diet play in the Kenyans' success? And, more importantly, could eating like the Kenyans help you run fast too?

Mike Kibe, a promising young Kenyan runner living in the United States, provided insights into Kenyans' typical eating habits. "We basically eat two meals a day: lunch and dinner," Kibe explained, "unless someone is training three times a day to get in shape. That runner will have something easily digested, such as bread and butter or two boiled eggs, following the first early-morning run, so they will be ready to go again a few hours later. Otherwise, we'll drink tea made with lots of milk and sugar before and after our first workout, as well as fruit, following the run, to settle our stomachs."

Lunch consists of more tea (one to two large cups), and a "light" meal of rice or potatoes topped with cabbage and other vegetables, as well as a few pieces of chicken. If they are hungry between meals, runners reach for more fruit—no snacks or sweet foods are kept in the house. Following the day's second training session, the runners look forward to a late dinner of generous portions of *ugali*, topped with a vegetable stew of sautéed greens and small pieces of beef. "At dinner we eat to repair our body tissues," Kibe shared, "as the body must have back what it lost. You must eat enough to have enough energy to train tomorrow—and that does not come from a spoonful of food."

So will eating like a Kenyan help your speed or stamina? Maybe not. Many people who study the success of Kenya's runners believe that one key to their success is being raised at a high elevation. In such an environment, the body obtains and uses oxygen more efficiently. Of course, eating mainly vegetables and fresh fruit as they do in Kenya, also will help you to lose weight. Are you ready to give up your hamburger and fries and other American fast foods, though?

One of the better-known Kenyan cuisines is *ugali*, a maize meal, similar to grits in the United States. Ugali is not

A woman grinds corn, or maize, that has traditionally been a large part of the Kenyans' diet. Is there a connection between such foods and skill at long-distance running?

grits, however, but is simply cornmeal cooked in boiling water until it has the same consistency and texture as bread dough. Because it is not very flavorful on its own, it is often eaten with saucy meals and dishes that have gravy. Take some ugali between two fingers and thumb and then scoop up some stew or vegetables and put them all together in your mouth. This way ugali is rather tasty. Perhaps you would like to try a genuine Kenyan dish. Here is the recipe for ugali.

Ugali

Ingredients

Maize (white corn flour or yellow cornmeal. The type of flour used—from white corn flour to yellow cornmeal)—determines the character of the ugali.

Water

Salt (optional)

Preparation

Put one cup of cold water in a medium-sized saucepan, and mixing continually, add one cup of corn flour and one teaspoon of salt. Bring to a boil over high heat and slowly mix in three cups of boiling water. Reduce to simmer, cover and cook for about five to eight minutes, mixing frequently to prevent sticking. The ugali is done when it pulls from the sides of the pan and does not stick. The finished product should look like stiff grits. Serve with vegetable beef broth, cream, sugar, syrup, or melted butter poured over it.

A NIGHT OUT

Kenyans living in cities such as Nairobi and Mombasa enjoy a "night on the town." Let's join them for an evening of partying! Be forewarned, of course, that the surroundings are not so safe and robbery is a real threat. One must be cautious even in New York or London, however, and most large cities are experiencing rising crime rates. When you go at night into the empty or deserted streets of the city, it is best to go in groups, or at least in pairs. Strangely enough, the area notorious for being most dangerous is probably the safest—the River Road area. This part of town constantly buzzes with activity. During the weekend, large crowds of people mill about on the streets often until the early morning hours. You are not likely to find trouble unless you ask for it, for example, by wearing conspicuously expensive jewelry. Take care, but have fun!

Before saying "goodbye" to Kenyan culture, let's visit one of the country's most famous culture groups—the Maasai cattle herders.

THE MAASAI

The Maasai are one of Kenya's best-known cultures. These tribal peoples are most directly related to the Turkana and Kalenjin who live near Lake Turkana in west central Kenya. They are a traditional pastoral people who are semi-nomadic and who practice a communal system of sharing with one another. Today, their way of life is being threatened. Large areas of their former grazing lands are today included in Kenya's national parks. Maasai routinely ignore both the park and international boundaries as they move their great cattle herds across the open savanna with the changing of the seasons. According to traditional land policies, no one should be denied access to natural resources such as water and land.

Traditionally, the Maasai diet is comprised of meat, milk, and blood from cattle. People drink blood on special occasions. It is given to a circumcised person, a woman who has given birth, and to the sick. Also, on a regular basis, drunken elders drink blood to ease intoxication and hangovers. However, its use in the traditional diet is diminishing due to reduction of livestock numbers.

More recently, the Maasai have grown dependent on food produced in other areas such as maize meal, rice, potatoes, and cabbage (known to the Maasai as goat leaves). Those who live near crop farmers have engaged in cultivation as their chief form of survival. In such areas, plot sizes generally are not large enough to contain herds of animals. Therefore, the Maasai are forced to farm. Maasai people traditionally frown upon this and believe that utilizing the land for crop farming is a crime against nature. Once you cultivate the land, it is no longer suitable for grazing.

The semi-nomadic lifestyle of the Maasai of herding cattle is slowly changing to more permanent ranching and crop farming.

Maasai society is full of ceremonies and celebrations. Every ceremony is a new life, they are rites of passage and every Maasai child is anxious to meet these stages of life. Circumcision, marriage, warrior graduation, and the milk ceremony are examples. Also, there is an abundance of rituals for young girls and boys. For example, boys and girls must undergo earlobe cutting and leg fire marks before circumcision. Most initiations concern men, although female initiations focus on circumcision and marriage. At initiation, men form age-sets and move with them through adulthood. Women do not have their own age-sets, but are recognized by that of their husbands.

This gives you just a small taste of the Maasai culture and their many unique customs. Unfortunately, the Maasai culture is under tremendous pressure. As the Maasai say, "it takes one day to destroy a house, but to build a new one will take months, perhaps years. If we destroy our way of life to construct a new one, it will take thousands of years." Sadly, this way of life, similar to the destroyed house, appears to be vanishing under the relentless wave of "progress" and modernization.

A scene of Nairobi, the capital city of a country whose population is relatively young compared to the United States. The life expectancy here is only about 47 years.

CHAPTER

5

Population and Life in Kenya's Provinces

I n this chapter, you will learn about Kenya's demographic (population) patterns and settlement, or the distribution of people about the country.

POPULATION

Today, Kenya's population numbers well over 30 million people (an estimated 31,138,735 in 2003). One striking feature of the country's population is its age structure. Fully 44% of the people are 14 years old or younger, whereas only a small 3% of the population is 65 or older. The huge percentage of young people means that Kenya's high rate of population growth no doubt will continue for decades. In the United States by contrast, only 21% of the population is aged 0–14, whereas 13% is older than 65. Thus Kenya has double the rate of young dependents (the population that is less than

15 years old) compared to the United States, but less than one-third the rate of old dependents (those older than 65 years). Clearly, Kenyans do not live as long as Americans. The average life expectancy for Kenya in mid-2002 was a mere 48 years, compared to 77 years for the United States. Moreover, whereas 74 out of every 1,000 children born in Kenya died before their first birthday, in the United States it was fewer than 7 per 1,000.

The total fertility rate (TFR) is the average number of children each woman has during her lifetime. Countries with high fertility rates have high rates of population growth. Kenya's fertility rate of 4.4 is more than twice the rate of the United States, which is only 2.1. In short, Kenyan women have on average two more children than American women, and thus the population grows more rapidly.

Population growth is a function of three factors: births, deaths, and net migration rates. The most common measure is the rate of natural increase, or RNI. This is simply the difference between the number of births per 1,000 population and the number of deaths per 1,000 population in any selected year. The number of births per 1,000 population is called the birthrate, and the number of deaths per 1,000 population is called the deathrate. Thus, for Kenya with a birthrate of 34 per 1,000 and a deathrate of 14 per 1,000, the rate of natural increase is 20 per 1,000 or 2%. For the United States, with a birthrate of 15 and a deathrate of 9, the rate of natural increase is only 6 per 1,000 or 0.6%. Kenya's rate of natural population increase is more than three times that of the United States.

For sub-Saharan Africa as a whole, with a birthrate of 40 and a deathrate of 15, the rate of natural population increase is 2.5%. This means that Kenya's population growth is lower than the average rate for Africa south of the Sahara. This is very encouraging, because rapid population growth usually makes it more difficult to provide a good quality of life for a country's people. Suppose, for example, that the population of school-going children doubled every ten years. In a poor country it might be difficult or even impossible to provide enough classroom space and well-prepared teachers. Can you imagine what would happen? Some teachers would have to teach twice as many children, classroom furniture would have to be shared, and resources such as books could become scarce. In fact, as we will see later in this book, all of these are already happening in Kenya. Let us stop to visit with Mary, a new mother.

Mary, a Kenyan farmer, has just had her third son. Her husband works in a distant city and visits the family only several weeks a year. He uses his earnings to support himself and to buy occasional essentials for the family. Mary tells an interviewer that her three children are enough to bring her happiness and so, today, at 29, she is having surgery that will make her infertile. She has only one cow and a small piece of land that cannot be further divided, so although she cannot give her children land, she can provide them with an education. Mary says she will not be able to afford to educate all three. Such attitudes are spreading in Kenya, where rapid population growth means insufficient food, health care, or employment. Before going further on our reading journey through Kenya, let's observe some local demographic competition.

KENYA, UGANDA, OR TANZANIA — WHO IS THE WINNER?

A friendly rivalry has always existed between Kenya and her two closest neighbors, Tanzania and Uganda. The competition is somewhat similar to that between brothers or sisters, to see who can run faster or score more goals. Since the British colonized all three countries, the friendly competition to determine the most superior of the countries started immediately after independence. It continues today. Let us see how they compare on selected population indicators.

Tanzania has the largest population, 37.2 million, and Uganda has the least, 24.7 million. Kenya, with 31.1 million, falls almost evenly between the two. Tanzania has a birthrate of

40 per 1,000 and a deathrate of 13 per 1,000. But Uganda has a birthrate of 48 per 1,000 and a deathrate of 18 per 1,000. Their rate of natural increase, thus, is 2.7 and 3.0 respectively. Kenya, you may recall, has a birthrate of 34 and deathrate of 14, or a RNI of 2.0%. Compared to Uganda and Tanzania, Kenya is the winner for low population growth.

When it comes to life expectancy, however, Kenya does not fare as well in the competition. Tanzania is the clear winner with a life expectancy of 52 years. Kenya, with a life expectancy of 48 years, places second in the competition and Uganda, with only 43 years, is last again.

Measuring income and wealth is another way to rank countries. Here, too, there are differences between the three competing countries. Can you guess who is the winner here? It is Uganda with a per capita gross national income purchasing power parity (GNI-PPP) (purchasing power compared to the U.S. dollar) of $1,210. Tanzania is the clear loser in this competition, with only $520 GNI-PPP. Kenya, again, falls in second place with a figure of $1,010. Compared to the United States, however, these are very poor countries indeed. In 2002, the average per capita gross national income in the U.S. was $34,100. It might be difficult to even imagine, but each American makes about as much in one year as 34 Kenyans!

DISTRIBUTION OF KENYA'S POPULATION

Kenya's capital city, Nairobi, has a population of approximately 1.5 million people. The other major towns are Mombasa, with 1 million, and Kisumu on Lake Victoria with about 400,000 people. Among the country's eight provinces, population distribution is quite uneven. The semiarid to desert northeast province is very sparsely populated. But, in the rich and fertile western province, population density is very high. Most Kenyans live in the highlands, where the climate is mild. In area, Kenya's provinces range from the tiny Nairobi province

Province	Capital	Area SQ KM	Area SQ MI	Population 2002	Population Density per SQ. MILE/KM
Central	Nyeri	13,176	5,087	4,527,700	890/2,305
Coast	Mombasa	83,603	32,279	2,728,800	84/220
Eastern	Embu	159,891	61,734	5,693,600	92/238
North Eastern	Garissa	126,902	48,997	473,200	10/26
Nyanza	Kisumu	16,162	6,240	5,152,300	826/2,139
Rift Valley	Nakuru	173,868	67,131	8,178,900	122/316
Western	Kakamega	8,360	3,228	3,765,300	1,166/3,020
Nairobi Area	Nairobi	684	264	2,564,500	9,714/25,150
Kenya	Nairobi	582646	224960	31,765,300	141/365

Table 1. Population Distribution in Kenya's Provinces

to the huge eastern and rift valley provinces. Table 1 presents the area and population breakdown by provinces.

Now that you know about the population and area of the provinces, you must be eager to know what they are like. Let us take a quick tour through each of Kenya's provinces. On the whirlwind tour of the country, you will encounter camels, crocodiles, and beautiful beaches. You also will visit beautiful towering mountains and hot, tropical lowlands. You will even meet some local people and get to visit a few homes. Let's begin the journey in the dry northeastern desert region.

North Eastern Province

The dry northeast, home to the north eastern province, is the most sparsely populated. Most of it is semidesert. Soils are sandy and, beside a few scattered thorny trees, there is little vegetation. Rainfall is rare and the dry season lasts all year.

During the few days a year when rain does fall, seasonal rivers can overflow their banks and roads often become impassable. Some parts of this remote region are almost inaccessible. Here, "Flying Doctor" services via airplane are used to supplement the meager health care available locally.

Because of the limited rainfall, farming is not feasible. Most people keep camels, cattle, sheep, and goats. They practice a nomadic lifestyle, moving from place to place seasonally in search of water and good pasture for their livestock. For food they depend on wild honey and milk and meat from their animals. Housing for these nomads is a simple framework of poles covered with panels of thatch and sheets of leather. The poles, coverings, household goods, milk gourds, water pots, pets, and children are loaded onto a camel when it is time for the next move. Many of the nomads are Muslims and are generally very friendly. The rather hostile environment in which they live contributes to their looking out for one another.

When you think about the north eastern province, think about camels, little rain, and sparse desert vegetation. After visiting this environment, perhaps you are ready for the beautiful beaches, lush tropical vegetation, and coconut palms of the coast province!

Coast Province

Beautiful stretches of sandy beach, coral reefs, starfish, prawns (shrimp), crabs, and seashells welcome you to coast province. The climate is hot and humid, but the sparkling beaches, cooled by sea breezes, keep the tourists coming. Tourist hotels and plantations of coconut, cashew nut, sisal (agave, used in making twine, rope, and other woven objects), and sugarcane line the coast road. Scuba diving is fast becoming popular and several marine parks draw divers and other tourists to the coast. Along the roadside, large mango trees shade marketplaces. The low, square houses are made of white and brown coral rock. Their roofs are thatched with coconut fronds (leaves).

Besides tourism, fishing is a major economic activity. Fishermen use mangrove poles to push dugout canoes through shallow water where they lay fish traps made of basketwork, with a funnel-shaped entrance. Islam is the dominant religion in coast province. Thus, Islamic festivals and ceremonies are commonplace here. Muslim women often wear the *burqa*, a traditional black, loose-fitting dress, with a black head covering.

Coast province provides an excellent example of what geographers call sequent occupancy. This term describes the layered cultural landscape that results after different cultures settle sequentially, each leaving its own unique cultural imprint on the land. First, traders from Arabia came to Kenya in sailing ships called *dhows*. They introduced the Islamic dome-shaped architecture as they built Arab towns with multistory housing, narrow streets, and mosques for Islamic worship. Later, the British and Portuguese built European-style homes and churches for Christian worship. Another British legacy was the Mombasa-Uganda railway. Finally, Asians came from India to work on the railway line. Taking up jobs as shopkeepers, clerks, and skilled workers, they introduced Indian architecture and culture, especially Hinduism.

Mombasa, the capital of coast province, is an island that is separated from the mainland by a sheltered, deep-water harbor. It is also a major African seaport, handling cargo for Kenya and its landlocked neighbors. Two of Kenya's biggest industries, an oil refinery and a cement factory, are located near the port. People from all over Kenya work at the ports, in the factories, and in the beach hotels. Many coastal people continue their traditional occupations, as farmers, fishermen, craftsmen, traders, and Islamic scholars.

The pace of life in Mombasa is suited to the hot climate. All the shops are quite small. They open in the morning, close for a long break during the heat of day, and open again during the cooler evening when shoppers and diners fill the streets. Coastal cooking is rich and varied, with a lot of fish and rice and many dishes cooked in coconut milk.

It's time to go already as the eastern region beckons us. But don't forget coast province with its scuba diving, coconuts, tourists, and midday *siesta*.

Eastern Province

Welcome to eastern province, perhaps the most diverse physical environment of Kenya. The natural landscape ranges from near-desert in the north to large expanses of prairie grasslands in the south. This is the home of the Maasai, the Kamba, the Meru and other tribes. Cattle are the most important possession of these people, providing milk, meat, and blood for food. To find good pasture and water for their animals, the Maasai walk very long distances. Lately, some Maasai have begun ranching and thus move less frequently.

Historically, most Maasai cattle herders lived in temporary houses with walls made of mud mixed with cow dung over a frame of poles. Women usually built and decorated these houses. Dung keeps the walls smooth and waterproof. Lately, staying in one place to enable children to attend school seems to be the preferred option. Many families have settled on farms, and are growing crops suited to dry land.

The many national parks and reserves in the eastern province attract a large number of tourists. Tourism, in fact, is the major economic activity in the region. It is the major source of revenue and employment for both men and women. Men work as game rangers, gatekeepers, tour guides and drivers; women sell snacks, animal carvings, and beaded jewelry to the tourists. Wildlife is abundant here. While on *safari*, you should see lions, leopards, zebras, gazelle, giraffes, black rhinos, and elephants.

Although there is much more to see in the eastern province, we must move on. We now leave the scenic homeland of the Maasai and their precious cattle, and visit central province.

The eastern province houses many national parks, game reserves, and large open lands perfect for grazing cattle.

Central Province

Central province is home to the Kenyan highlands and the heart of Kenya agriculture. The fertile volcanic soil that originated from Mount Kenya when it was an active volcano covers the area and provides excellent growing conditions for many types of crops. The area is well watered and the cool temperatures make it ideal. Large agricultural estates and many subsistence-farming communities exist side by side.

Among subsistence-farming families, children usually fetch water from a stream, spring, or tap some distance away. Because family farms are scattered all over, most children walk long distances to school, sometimes more than three miles each way. Can you imagine coming back from school and having to go fetch water, carrying it a long distance in a bucket which, when filled, may weigh 25–30 pounds and is carried on your head?

A live hedge fences the home compounds, or *shambas*.

The central province's climate and soil are perfect for growing cash crops like the vegetables these women are selling at market.

The houses and sheds are round or square, with roofs of thatch or iron sheets. Farm animals kept at such shambas include dairy cows, a few goats, sheep, donkeys, a flock of chickens, and a guard dog. Cash crops, such as coffee, and food crops, such as maize, bananas and potatoes, are grown for family meals or sold locally. Many small farmers have market gardens where they grow vegetables for the market.

Maize (corn) is the staple food. It is dried and then ground into flour that is used to prepare meals. Breakfast may be porridge made from maize flour, although most people prefer millet flour. For lunch or supper, maize flour is used to make ugali, which is usually eaten with green vegetables or stew.

It is time to leave central province, but remember the Kenyan highlands and agricultural productivity. Oh, and don't forget the time when you fell on your way back from the stream where you had gone to fetch water. You got drenched, lost your water, and had to go back to fill the bucket again. You were late for school that day, but your teacher understood!

Rift Valley Province

Rift valley, Kenya's largest province, presents a fascinating physical landscape. Traveling from the coast region to western Kenya, just after the town of Limuru, the landscape suddenly changes as the elevation drops nearly 1,000 feet (300 meters). The western side of the Great Rift Valley stands like a massive wall, while the valley floor remains flat, broken only by occasional long and narrow lakes occupying the bottom of the trench. Evidence of old volcanoes is everywhere and includes numerous hot springs, steam jets, and geysers. Before you go for a quick swim in the natural hot spring, test the water temperature. In some places, it is known to exceed 570°F (300°C). This natural resource is now being tapped to produce geothermal power.

Lake Turkana is the largest of Kenya's rift valley lakes. It is quite shallow, slightly alkaline, and full of fish. Fishing, in fact, is the main livelihood of local residents. It also has a sizeable population of Nile crocodiles. While the volcanic soil of the rift valley is very fertile, rainfall is low. Areas with adequate rainfall, or irrigation systems, have exceptionally high agricultural productivity.

We still have more to see on our tour of this fascinating country. Let's visit the huge Amboseli National Park. Here, we will see ostriches, impala, elephants, buffalo, monkeys, kudus, and even warthogs. As we leave, remember the rift valley. If geologists are right, someday this will be an ocean.

Western Province

Western province has ideal conditions for plant cultivation. The area has deep rich soils, adequate rainfall, mild temperatures, and abundant sunshine all year round. Bamboo forests encircle the high slopes of Mount Elgon, while forests of native cedar and olive abound on the lower slopes. Below the extensive mountain forests are plantations of pine and cypress trees. Timber mills and paper-making factories exploit the softwood in these plantations. Many houses here are built of wood.

The farms in this region are usually small. Subsistence agriculture predominates, with the surplus being sold in the numerous nearby markets found along the roads and railway lines that link the region. Eldoret, one of these market towns, has become a major commercial center. Among its major industries are cotton, wool, synthetic textiles, and food processing. We must now move on to Lake Victoria. But don't forget the lumber and wood products, small farms and market towns, or large plantations you visited in western province.

Nyanza Province

Welcome to Nyanza, the province that borders Lake Victoria. Nyanza province gets its name from the Swahili word for lake. Lake-centered activity dominates the local economy, especially fishing and boat building. Wooden boats and hand-woven nets are used to catch Tilapia, the most popular fish, or the huge Nile perch.

Thunderstorms occur frequently over the lake. For example, the Kisii highlands in southwestern Kenya get about 250 thunderstorm days a year. Due to the abundance of rainfall, the hills and the flat lowlands near the lake are the most densely settled rural areas in Kenya. A large variety of food crops can be grown here including millet, maize, cassava, and bananas. Some of the millet grown here is used to brew a popular local beer called *busaa*.

Kisumu, the capital of Nyanza province, is Kenya's main lake port. Numerous churches, mosques, and schools serve the dense population. Local culture is very vibrant. While western clothes are usually worn, an incredible collection of costumes is displayed for dances and ceremonies. Some of the more popular ones include robes of animal skins, masks from woven fibers, headdresses, horns, and shells. The musical instruments used during such ceremonies vary from bells, rattles, and horns to eight-stringed harp.

As you leave Nyanza, remember fishing and thunderstorms.

Don't forget the beautiful, inexpensive mask that you bought. Now let's go to Nairobi, the national capital.

Nairobi

Nairobi, Kenya's national capital, is a multicultural city of about 1.5 million people. Many of these are rural migrants. Both Swahili and English are spoken. Churches, mosques, and various temples cater to the wide array of religious beliefs. Restaurants serve an amazing variety of food from Indian curry to Chinese, Arabian, and European cuisine.

Like other African cities, Nairobi has its share of wealthy residential areas and sprawling slums. Houses range from beautiful mansions set in large gardens, to crowded row houses, four-story blocks of flats, and shacks made of wood and plastic sheets. In the early stages of its colonial development, Nairobi catered specifically to Europeans. Africans, Europeans, and Asians were segregated based on occupation and income and Europeans controlled most of the economy and administration. Asians worked as merchants and artisans, while Africans took up the menial jobs. Traffic congestion is a major problem in Nairobi. Most wealthy people drive to work. For the rest, a variety of public transport is available, including matatus.

Matatus

Matatus, individually owned minibuses, are by far the most common means of transportation in Kenya. They are affordable and accessible. They leave from designated spots called stages. Passengers get seated, and then the matatu leaves when it is full. Matatus can also be caught from the road. If one is passing, stick out your arm with your palm down. This is the sign you want to be picked up. If the vehicle is not full, the driver will swerve over to let you in, regardless of whether they are doing it on a roundabout (traffic circle) or a highway. With blaring loud music, these brightly painted vehicles careen along the roads seemingly in a frenzy.

Taxis known as *matatus* are easy to identify with their lively colors and loud music. Police officers frequently stop overloaded matatus to demand bribes in exchange for not issuing a traffic ticket.

At least two people run every matatu, a driver and a tout (*makanga*) who usually is a young man dressed in the current fad. A driver's job is self-explanatory, but the work of a makanga needs a bit of explanation. First, they are mostly male. In fact, the authors have never seen a female makanga. Their job involves hanging out of the sliding door with the vehicle in motion while trying to coax riders on and announcing its destination very loudly and very fast. This is probably the most enjoyable part of their job because it invariably involves flirting, persuading, and simply looking "cool." Their other tasks include collecting fares and signaling the driver (by banging on the roof or tapping a coin on a window) when a stop is requested. They also open and close the sliding door for passengers and help to squish them and their belongings into the interior of the matatu. It is a coveted job for teenagers, and those who are good at it enjoy a lot of prestige.

Kenyans say that a matatu is never full, and unfortunately, this is usually true. No matter how many people, goats, and chickens are crammed into a matatu, the driver will always stop for more people and the makanga will shove them in. This makes for unsafe conditions and slow progress. Several times a day, the drivers cough up bribes to police who pull them over for cramming more than 20 people into minivans designed to carry 7.

Sometimes there are several matatus en route to the same destination, so makangas will "fight" over you. One may even grab your luggage and force you to follow him to his matatu. They can be very aggressive and rude, so never let a makanga take your bag. Make your own decision about which vehicle to take. At major stages, you pay for a ticket before you get on a matatu. It is common, however, to be asked for your money after the matatu is on its way. It is always a good idea to ask what the fare is before entering the matatu, also ask other customers what they are paying. Some makanga may try to cheat you!

So did you enjoy your ride? Don't forget your luggage. And, please watch out for the other matatus that are fast approaching your stop. You could get run over. Be careful, you still have much more of Kenya to see and to experience.

Kenyan President Daniel arap Moi was notorious for corruption and bribery. Here he receives a check for 1 million Kenyan shillings ($12,600) from the Armed Forces commanders.

6

Kenyan Politics and Economy

K enya gained independence on December 12, 1963. Jomo Kenyatta, a member of the predominant Kikuyu tribe and head of the Kenya African National Union (KANU), became its first president. The minority party, Kenya African Democratic Union (KADU), representing a coalition of small tribes that had feared dominance by larger ones, dissolved itself in 1964 and joined KANU. Thus, there was no opposition party.

A TURBULENT BEGINNING

The first decade of independence was full of disputes among ethnic groups, particularly between the Kikuyu and the Luo. Many Europeans and Asians voluntarily left the country. Their land was distributed to a large number of rural Africans who did not have farms. Kenyatta chose ministers from different tribes to ensure fair representation and avoid charges of tribalism. He also tried to win support of white settlers, because the economy depended on their exports.

Unfortunately, the Kenyatta government did not tolerate criticism. A small but significant socialist-leaning opposition party, the Kenya People's Union (KPU), was formed in 1966. Jaramogi Oginga Odinga, a former vice president and a Luo elder led it. Following KPU's criticism of the Kenyan government, the party was banned in 1969 and its leader was detained. After 1969, while Jomo Kenyatta was president, no new opposition parties were formed and KANU remained the only political party.

Sadly, the political record of independent Kenya is marred by a trail of blood from political assassinations. Those who openly opposed the government did not live long. Usually, the assassins and their accomplices were never caught. For example, Tom Mboya, a leading government official and potential successor to President Kenyatta, was assassinated in 1969. Mboya was one of the most brilliant leaders Africa has ever produced. While someone was tried and executed for his murder, most Kenyans believe that the real people behind the crime escaped justice. Similarly, the foreign minister, Robert Ouko was assassinated in 1990. This crime, too, was never solved. Such ruthless silencing of opponents led to further domestic unrest. Kenyatta died in 1978. Corruption and favoritism were the major characteristics of his government.

LIFE AFTER KENYATTA

After Kenyatta's death in 1978, Vice President Daniel arap Moi succeeded him as president. Moi promoted "Africanization" of industry by placing limits on foreign ownership and extending credit to African investors. He resisted and ruthlessly crushed calls for democracy. In June 1982, the National Assembly amended the constitution to officially make Kenya a one-party state. Kenya remained a one-party state until 1992.

Rifts and dissension characterized Moi's rule. He took criticism badly and viciously suppressed dissent wherever it occurred, including disrupting universities. When forces loyal to Moi put down a coup attempt by the Kenyan Air Force in 1982, the air force was disbanded and replaced by a new unit. Rioting erupted in 1988 after several outspoken proponents of multiparty democracy were arrested.

While winds of democratic change swept across much of Africa during the late 1980s and early 1990s, international aid for Kenya was suspended. The International Monetary Fund (IMF), the World Bank, and other potential donors demanded multiparty democracy as a condition for further aid. Bowing to pressure at home and abroad, the legislature passed a constitutional amendment legalizing multiparty democracy in 1991. Much to Moi's delight, however, the opposition party was unable to agree on a leader and split into three parties. In 1992, in the first multiparty election since independence, Moi won another five-year term. However, some rather unusual people were elected to office in 1992, including a woman named Charity Kaluki Ngilu.

Woman Dares to Challenge Moi

Charity Kaluki Ngilu was washing dishes in her kitchen in Kitui, about 73 miles from Nairobi, when she saw a group of women approaching her house with leafy branches in their hands. She had worked with them to build better water and health facilities in their town. While drying her hands on her apron, Mrs. Ngilu answered the knock on her door. The women asked her to run for parliament in Kenya's first multiparty elections. "You are joking," Charity told them. But they were serious.

Not wanting to let them down, Mrs. Ngilu ran for parliament. It was a major turning point! She easily defeated the government party's incumbent candidate, although she had practically none of her opponent's resources. She went on to be an exemplary political representative and continuously criticized the Moi government for doing little or nothing for the poor, especially women.

In 1997, she announced that she would run for the presidency. As the first woman to run for Kenya's highest office, most people thought she was joking but she was not. She campaigned very hard but was not successful. Charity placed fifth, receiving about 360,000 votes, compared to 2,400,000 votes received by Moi. She could not match the huge amounts of money Moi used to buy votes. In Kenya, most women do not vote at all, and men are not likely to support female candidates. Many men supported her because they were tired of President Moi's corrupt and inefficient government, they believed she could make more lasting and important changes.

Although Mrs. Ngilu did not win the elections, she made a very important point with her campaign. She showed that Kenya did not belong to men alone. She called for changes in the unfair laws that allowed the president to arrest and imprison his political opponents and thus cripple the opposition. Mrs. Ngilu demonstrated that even in Africa, it helps to dream in a big way.

WOMEN IN KENYAN POLITICS

Historically, participation of women in Kenyan national politics has been minimal. KANU, which has been in power since independence in 1963, only appointed the country's first female cabinet minister in 1995. During the last term of Moi's 24-year rule, the 25-member cabinet was made up entirely of men. Only 8 of 224 members of parliament were women. That is only 3% even though women constitute 54% of the voters.

Today, things are changing rapidly. The number of women running for parliamentary seats increased from 48 in 1997 to about 80 in 2002. A total of eight women were elected to parliament on various party tickets. Currently, there are 15 women serving in parliament. This number is still small in proportion to parliament's total of 210 seats, but women leaders are still happy

Charity Ngilu rides on her way, in 1997, to officially register for an upcoming campaign. She was the first woman presidential candidate in Kenya's history.

that the NARC government is showing signs of commitment to improving the status of women. In fact, in 2003, three women were serving as cabinet ministers.

DANIEL ARAP MOI'S LEGACY

When Moi became president he took the motto *Nyayo*, Swahili for "footsteps," indicating his wish to follow in Kenyatta's path. Over the years, Moi consolidated his hold on power and surrounded himself with a group of supportive "yes men" who constantly sang his praises. During his rule, taking bribes and paying off government workers to obtain even small services such as parking became a daily part of life. Moi, himself, became larger than life. His picture was on the country's currency and hung from the wall of nearly every store. Streets, schools and airports were named after him. And he instituted a national holiday—Moi Day.

What do you think Kenyans thought as they celebrated Moi Day, or as they walked along Moi Avenue on their way to pick up their children from Moi Academy, or counted their money imprinted with Moi's face? President Daniel arap Moi, whose "big man"-style rule was characterized by injustice, repression, and greed, appeared invincible. Yet, he ruled Kenya for 24 long years. Finally, in December 2002, the Moi era was over. The constitution limited him to only two terms. It was time for a new beginning.

END OF AN ERA

In June 2001, a cabinet reshuffle put members of the second largest opposition group, National Development Party (NDP), into key cabinet slots forming an unprecedented coalition government. In March 2002, KANU merged with the NDP. In response to the KANU-NDP merger, several leading opposition parties came together under the umbrella of the National Alliance for Change (NAC). President Moi picked Uhuru Kenyatta, the son of founding president Jomo Kenyatta, to succeed him and contest the presidency as the KANU candidate. At least three other candidates from KANU, though, declared their interest to run for president against his preferred successor.

Quickly, six opposition parties launched an umbrella party, the National Rainbow Coalition (NARC), with Mwai Kibaki as the leader and presidential candidate. NARC consisted of opposition politicians and a large group of ruling party politicians who were unhappy at Mr. Moi's promotion of the young and inexperienced candidate, Uhuru Kenyatta. Kibaki, himself, was Moi's vice president from 1978 to 1988. He also was the country's longest-serving finance minister, holding the post from 1969 to 1982.

Nevertheless, perhaps due to Moi's unpopularity at this time, the hastily assembled coalition won a decisive victory in the December 2002 elections. Kibaki and his NARC party were declared the winner, receiving 63% of the vote. Moreover, in the

210-seat legislature, the Rainbow alliance captured 122 seats, KANU won 52, and smaller parties won the remaining positions.

MWAI KIBAKI, KENYA'S THIRD PRESIDENT

Mwai Kibaki was born in 1931 on the slopes of Mount Kenya. He is Kikuyu, a member of Kenya's largest tribe. After studying in Uganda and London, he became a professor, but in the early 1960s gave it up to help in Kenya's struggle for independence. He helped draft Kenya's constitution, was elected as a member of parliament (MP) in 1963, and has held a seat ever since. He was finance minister during the 1970s and vice president for much of the 1980s, serving under the country's first president, Jomo Kenyatta, and then his successor, President Moi. When the ban on opposition parties was lifted in 1991, Mr. Kibaki left KANU to found the Democratic party, which he still leads. He finished third in the first multiparty elections in 1992 and finished a close second in the 1997 elections.

When Mwai Kibaki was elected president, he became the third person to lead the country since it gained independence from Britain in 1963. More importantly, Kibaki's party, NARC, ended the KANU party's 40-year hold on national politics. At his inauguration, Kibaki declared: "I am inheriting a country which has been badly ravaged by years of misrule and ineptitude." Kibaki promised to fight corruption in a nation where a system of patronage and bribes has severely damaged state institutions.

The smooth election defied widespread fears that it would be rigged, as voting had been in 1992 and 1997. Election observers from the European Union and the Carter Center in the United States said the election sent an important message to other African nations, where transitions are often fragile and frequently lead to civil wars. While Kenyans celebrate, the future remains quite unstable. In Kenya as elsewhere, a very close relationship exists between government and economy.

KENYA'S ECONOMIC HISTORY

Today, Kenya's economy is in trouble. During the 1960s and 1970s, annual economic growth reached a booming 8%. By 2001, however, it had plummeted to -3%. The majority of Kenyans live below the poverty level and the average Kenyan makes about $1 a day. Because of mass unemployment, and resulting frustration and poverty, violent crime—including armed robbery, carjackings, and murder—is increasingly frequent in Nairobi and other major towns. In 1999, the World Bank and the International Monetary Fund (IMF) classified Kenya as one of 52 "heavily indebted poor countries." Basic infrastructure, such as roads, telephones, railways and electricity, were in considerable disrepair. It was estimated that it would take one billion dollars to get the nation's roads back into good working order. How did this happen?

After independence, Kenya promoted rapid economic growth through public investment, small-scale agricultural production, and incentives for private (often foreign) industrial investment. Gross domestic product (GDP) grew at an annual average of 6.6% from 1963 to 1973. Agricultural production grew by 4.7% annually during the same period, as previously landless Kenyans received land from redistributed white-owned estates.

Between 1974 and 1990, however, Kenya's economic performance declined. Inappropriate agricultural policies, inadequate credit, and poor international terms of trade contributed to the decline in agriculture. The oil shortages of the early 1970s, collapse of the East African Economic Community, and other external factors caused a huge slowdown in growth. The "coffee boom" brought economic growth in 1976 and 1977. During most of the 1980s, the economy was stable with annual growth around 5%. By 1989, however, growth began to decline as a result of poor weather, regional conflict bringing an influx of refugees, bad government, and a global recession that lowered demand for Kenya's traditional export products.

A farmer in 1999 cleans coffee beans with a bow and arrow at his side to defend himself. The coffee industry was very turbulent after farmers stormed cooperative factories and accused the managers of corruption.

From 1991 to 1993, Kenya experienced its worst economic performance since independence. Growth in GDP stagnated, and agricultural production shrank at an annual rate of nearly 4%. Inflation reached a record 100% in August 1993, and the government's budget deficit was over 10% of GDP. Under pressure, the government adopted the World Bank- and IMF-sponsored program of economic reform and liberalization (structural adjustment) in 1993. As part of this program, the government abolished price controls, import licensing, and foreign exchange controls. Some government-owned companies were privatized. The number of civil servants was cut and conservative fiscal and monetary policies were implemented. From 1994 to 1996, Kenya's economic growth averaged just over 4% a year and inflation remained under control.

Economic growth slowed after 1997, averaging only 1.5% between 1997–2000. In 1997, political violence damaged the tourist industry. Fed up with the government's failure to maintain economic reform and address public sector corruption, the IMF suspended desperately needed loans. This prompted other donors to withdraw their support as well. Severe drought in 1999 and 2000 caused water and energy rationing and reduced agricultural productivity. Kenya has so much potential, yet today it is one of the world's poorest countries. Kenya is a sad example of what can happen when a country is poorly governed for a long period.

KENYA'S ECONOMIC STRUCTURE

Kenya's economic structure has changed considerably since independence in 1963. Agriculture remains the backbone of the economy. But its share in overall GDP has declined from nearly 40% in the 1960s to about 20% by 2001. Over the same period, the contribution of the service sector increased from 39% to 62%. The share of industry has remained unchanged at about 20% since independence.

Kenya has East Africa's most industrially developed service economy. The service sector accounts for about 62% of Kenya's GDP. This category includes the various services provided by the restaurant, hotel, and safari industries, and also government services. Industry, which includes mining and construction, contributed 19% of GDP in 2000. Kenya's chief manufactures include food products, beverages, tobacco, textiles and clothing, rubber products, transport equipment, printed materials, and petroleum, and chemicals. Mining employs only a small number of Kenya's workers. The 1997 discovery of valuable titanium and zircon deposits bordering the Indian Ocean offers potential economic benefit.

Petroleum is Kenya's major source of energy. Unfortunately, the country's entire supply is imported. Electricity is the second most important energy source. Some 71% of Kenya's electricity is generated by hydroelectric plants in the Tana River basin, in the Turkwel River gorge, and in neighboring Uganda. Kenya also has a geothermal station and an oil-burning facility that produce electricity.

Kenya has one of the most extensive transportation networks in East Africa. Railways connect the major cities, and the road network is substantial, although some 80% remains unpaved and in poor shape. Mombasa, the major seaport, serves Uganda, Rwanda, and other landlocked countries in the region. Kisumu is the major port on Lake Victoria and river transport is limited. International airports are located at Nairobi, Mombasa, and Eldoret with Kenya Airways as the national airline. The main forms of public transportation in Kenya are buses, matatus, and taxis.

RESCUING KENYA'S ECONOMY

The new government of Mwai Kibaki has promised to fight corruption and rebuild ties with international lenders and donors. President Kibaki's government has created an anti-corruption authority and passed a law defining economic crimes. He has also ordered public officials to declare their wealth, and has created a new department to oversee the campaign to clean up government corruption.

Kenya's finance minister has announced a payment freeze on all government contracts while the ministry reviews its spending priorities. The government wants to ensure that none of the payments involve bribes or fraudulent claims. The IMF reviewed Kenya's progress in early 2003 and promised to restore the much-needed lending program. Since its independence, Kenya has often suffered from poor management and corruption and a stagnant economy. If blessed with a stable government and honesty in business and politics, Kenya has the potential of becoming the engine of East Africa's economic growth.

Tourism, a bright spot on the Kenyan economy, takes advantage of the country's beautiful sights and wild animals. The tourism industry is being threatened, however, by the fear of terrorism and crime.

Life in Kenya Today

T hree words summarize much of contemporary Kenyan life: tourism, corruption, and terrorism.

TOURISM

Kenya is a tourist haven. With nearly 50 national parks and game reserves, it is the best known and most popular safari destination in all of Africa. Wildlife is not the country's only tourist attraction. Beautiful tropical beaches and snowcapped mountain ranges also draw sightseers, as do the famous rift valley, geysers, and hot springs. Kenya's coastline is famous for its hundreds of miles of clean, sandy, palm-fringed coral beaches, lapped by the clear, blue waters of the Indian Ocean. Its coasts offer intriguing cultural and historical surroundings including picturesque old Arab towns and the ruins of sixteenth-century Portuguese settlements. Miles of unspoiled beaches, protected from sharks by the great coral barrier reef, provide an excellent setting for scuba diving and game fishing. New cottage-style hotels draw on local architectural styles and decor and offer an international standard of luxury.

For most visitors, however, Kenya means a safari across the savannah to view the country's abundant and varied wildlife. In the past, many people hunted big game animals. Today, however, most tourists on safari do their hunting with a camera and few are disappointed. The country is home to vast numbers of elephants, lions, leopards, rhinoceros, cheetahs, giraffes, hyena, and hippopotamus. There are also huge herds of grazing wildebeest, antelope, gazelle, waterbuck, and impala. Monkeys and many other animals also can be found in their natural habitat. Most of the 1,500 or so species listed for the eastern half of tropical Africa are found in Kenya. The largest concentration of flamingoes on earth is located in lakes Nakuru and Bogoria in the rift valley. There is so much to see in Kenya, let's take a quick tour of the country's major parks.

Lake Turkana

Lake Turkana is home to a huge population of crocodiles. Because the lake's waters are heavily alkaline, a trait that makes their skin worthless, these crocodiles live in peace without fear of poachers. Consequently, some of them grow to monstrous sizes. Are you thinking about taking a dip in the inviting waters? Think again! Swimming with crocodiles is risky business. Fishing, of course, is safe and fish are plentiful. Among its many species is the Nile perch, the world's largest freshwater fish that can weigh up to 400 pounds.

Two national parks are in the Lake Turkana region and both are home to crocodiles. Central Island, with three volcanic cones, is also the world's largest crocodile breeding ground. South Island is also volcanic and full of crocodiles. A thrilling way to see the crocodiles is by night. Just shine a flashlight over the water, and watch their eyes reflect a deep, luminous red over great distances.

Maasai Mara Game Reserve

Maasai Mara is the Kenyan portion of the great Serengeti Plains of Tanzania. It is one of the world's most astounding game parks. The most popular attraction here has always been the migration of enormous herds of wildebeest (1.3 million) and zebra (400,000). Searching for water, the herds move north from the Serengeti in Tanzania in May or June, arriving in Maasai Mara around mid-July. They return south beginning in mid-October. Accompanying the herds, of course, are their natural predators. Numerous lions, for example, follow the wildebeest to Maasai Mara. Don't get too close, you could become lunch!

Maasai Mara is most spectacular during the migration. But even when the wildebeest are in the south, it is Kenya's most spectacular game reserve. This is because an incredible array of different species of antelope, elephant, leopard, cheetah, rhino, giraffe, buffalo—virtually all of Africa's big game animals— can be found in abundance.

Ecotourism

Ecotourism—tourism that minimizes the human impacts on natural surroundings such as plant and animal life—is growing very rapidly. In addition to being more environmentally sensitive, ecotourism encourages local communities to conserve their wild surroundings. Ecotourists respect and promote local culture and understand the value and fragility of native land and resources. Such sustainable tourism is clearly the wave of the future.

Who are the Tourists?

On average, about one million tourists visit Kenya each year, most of whom are Europeans. The United Kingdom and

Germany are Kenya's top two tourism markets, followed by Switzerland, Italy, and the United States. More people visit Kenya from Britain than any other country, about 80,000 in an average year. Kenya is also a popular destination for Israelis.

Tourists who flock to Kenya's beaches and game reserves contribute approximately 12% of Kenya's economy and provide employment for about a half million people. Of these people, 300,000 work directly in the industry, while 200,000 work in related fields. Although tourism is a major source of foreign exchange, it is also extremely sensitive to political and social instability. Today, tourism is declining in Kenya due to ethnic riots, increasing crime in cities and tourist areas, and most recently, terrorism.

CORRUPTION

Kenya has been called a "Country of Bribes." Nothing is blamed more frequently for the country's stagnation than rampant corruption and patronage. In international surveys of corruption, Kenya is always featured prominently. One result of the country's poor standing is that key potential contributors to the country's economy have been unwilling to become involved in business ventures. Others have been unwilling to release much-needed financial aid. Political analysts say corruption is woven through every element of Kenyan society. In fact, giving or getting "a little something" to get through each day is inevitable. Without a bribe, it is difficult if not impossible for Kenyans to get a job, receive proper hospital care, obtain a driver's license, have phone lines installed, or even be able to pay bills.

Corruption is so much a part of the culture that in 2001 the most popular song in Kenya was "Country of Bribes." "If you're sick in the hospital or you lose your identity card, to get anything done in Kenya you have to pay a bribe," go the lyrics, written by Eric Wainaina, a young pop star and television celebrity.

In Mombasa, Kenyans liked to joke that the letters in Moi's name stand for "My Own Interest." Under Moi's leadership, such state services as education, trash collection, and road repair depended on a patronage system. Political analysts say that as Moi became less popular, money became the means for securing loyalty. He was not concerned with performance but with survival, and he rewarded those who helped him survive. Thus, bribery and patronage increased greatly.

Corruption has undermined the efficient allocation of economic resources. It also has destroyed investor confidence and greatly increased the cost of doing business in Kenya. International agencies such as the World Bank and the International Monetary Fund are withholding hundreds of millions of dollars earmarked for Kenya until corruption is under control. When the IMF suspended a $220 million loan in 1997, it said it was doing so because of "absurd and arguably unnecessary donor rituals." Much of these bribes were funneled to Moi from family members and friends. In 2001, Nairobi City Council officials found that hundreds of "ghost" workers — many of them distant relatives of Moi, or friends with connections — collected city paychecks, but were not officially employed. Thus, when phones don't work, the electricity goes out, or roads become full of deep potholes, the funds meant to maintain these services have usually gone into someone's pocket. Therefore, it often takes a bribe to get a job or run a business.

Some observers blame the terrorist attacks on the U.S. Embassy in Nairobi in 1998 and the Paradise Hotel in Mombasa in 2002 on the fact that weapons can easily be smuggled into the country with a bribe. Some people, of course, benefit tremendously from corruption and want the tradition to continue. It will be extremely difficult, and take strong and honest leadership to change this habit.

Cultural Explanations for Kenya's Corruption

In traditional African society, successful people were expected to share their wealth with their family and tribe. Society pressured those in positions of authority to "help" younger or less well-placed kinsmen to obtain similar or higher positions. Thus, it was not the most qualified person who got a job, but the most well-connected one. Consequently, it is normal for people from the extended family or tribe to approach politicians or academics for help in obtaining a job or scholarship.

This traditional practice is based on local cultural values and stands in sharp conflict with western ways of conducting affairs. Githongo, head of the Kenya branch of Transparency International, an international anticorruption watchdog group, put it this way: "So if the second cousin of your uncle's brother has been made an assistant minister of the environment, then you are riding the gravy train and aren't about to overthrow the government." Unfortunately this system consumes the state and undermines its institutions.

Similarly, another traditional value—reciprocity—is at stake. Dignity demands that the beneficiary of a favor should give something back in exchange. It also seems perfectly normal to give someone a gift today, in anticipation of asking for a favor tomorrow. Thus, some people do not see corruption as being harmful, especially those who benefit from it. The roots of bribery and corruption run very deep. Is there a solution?

Rooting out Bribery and Corruption

When Kibaki became Kenya's president, he faced a seemingly endless list of problems. The list included: inadequate health care; massive unemployment; a struggling public education system; and a shattered infrastructure of rocky roads, sporadic electricity, and bad telephones. Some Kenyans wondered where he should begin. Many say the answer is simple: stop corruption!

President Kibaki and his team plan to tackle the problem of corruption from the top. Kibaki has promised to publicly declare his wealth—something Moi never did. This could set a trend toward stopping corruption in everyday life. Leaders of Kibaki's NARC have announced plans to form a national forgiveness and reconciliation team that would offer anyone

A taxi designed to hold 7 passengers was stopped by a policeman for carrying 19. He demanded a common bribe but the passengers refused!

charged with stealing money from the government a chance to avoid prosecution by giving the money back. There also are plans to form committees to combat corruption and patronage in the police department and court system.

While these plans offer hope, rooting out corruption is not going to happen overnight. In fact, recent events suggest that it may not happen at all. During the election campaign, candidates continued the practice of handing out money for what Kenyans commonly call "our daily bread," a bribe for their votes. In the rural village of Mbeere, in the impoverished eastern province of the country, Uhuru Kenyatta's sister gave out "tea," the local name for a bribe, on Christmas Day. Families lined up for the equivalent of $2.50, in a country where most people live on a dollar a day. Can you blame them? Should the practice be stopped? If so, who will feed them?

TERRORISM

Past presidential elections in Kenya have been so violent that they usually scared away many tourists. The latest election,

A bomb in 1998 targeted the U.S. Embassy in Nairobi. Rescue workers look through debris of a nearby collapsed office building searching for survivors.

however, was different. It was not accompanied by violence. Unfortunately, this smooth transition of government was not sufficient to keep tourists coming. Today, there is another reason to worry—terrorism. Because of recent terrorist attacks on Kenya's coast, tourists are staying away in droves.

In 1998, Kenya was rocked by the attack on the United States embassy in Nairobi, which was blamed on Osama bin Laden. Some 219 people were killed and another 5,000 were wounded. Twelve other people were killed in a simultaneous attack in neighboring Tanzania. During the trial of those persons charged with the bombing of the Nairobi embassy, a witness said that two of the men involved in the crime lived in Kenya. They were part of an Al Qaeda terrorist cell in the country.

Four years later, on November 28, 2002, a car bomb detonated at the Israeli-owned Paradise Hotel, killing 16 people. Three were Israeli tourists (who were the targets), three were the bombers, and ten were Kenyans caught in the middle. Once again, Osama bin Laden's Al Qaeda claimed responsibility. At the same time, shoulder-launched missiles were used in an unsuccessful attempt to shoot down an Israeli charter aircraft as it left Mombasa. Although they are not the targets, Kenyans suffer the worst devastation from these attacks.

These recent terrorist attacks, together with the 1998 embassy bombing, have affected the tourism industry. American tourist arrivals declined from 311,170 in 2000 to 294,724 in 2001, and show continuing decline in 2002 and into 2003. Flights to the airport in Mombasa and cruise-ship arrivals have similarly fallen. It appears that, for now at least, American tourists are either staying home, or traveling to safer destinations.

Why Kenya? Why Mombasa?

Poverty, weak borders, corruption, and inept police make Kenya vulnerable to terrorist attacks. Kenya does not have a sophisticated security apparatus for dealing with attacks by groups like Al Qaeda. It is particularly vulnerable because of its long and porous borders with Tanzania, Uganda, Sudan, Somalia, and Ethiopia. For such a poor country, these borders are hard to police. The border with Somalia is particularly troublesome. For years, Somali armed bands known as *shiftas*, have been smuggling everything from ivory to weapons. Kenya has been unable to stop this illegal trade. Furthermore, ten years of conflict and instability in Somalia has made weapons easily available in its border areas. This makes it very easy for Muslim extremist groups such as Al Qaeda to bring weapons, including portable antiaircraft missiles, into the country.

Corruption, Kenya's omnipresent problem, is another contributory factor. Importing illegal goods is easy in the port of Mombasa. Drugs, weapons, and even endangered animals are easily smuggled into the country. All it takes is some *kitu kidogo*—Swahili for "a little something." Most customs officers get paid less than $100 a month and therefore find it difficult to refuse a bribe. Much of the illegal contraband is smuggled aboard merchant ships and dhows, large wooden sailing vessels that ply the waters of the Indian Ocean from Asia to Africa.

Finally, the huge Muslim population in coast province is another factor. The area around Mombasa has strong, centuries-old trading relations with Arab states in the Persian Gulf and on the Arabian Peninsula. Islamic radicalism has been spreading in the coast province for at least a decade. Following the embassy bombing and the search for Al Qaeda cells after September 11, 2001, Muslim groups in Mombasa and Nairobi staged demonstrations. They were protesting what they believed to be persecution of Muslims. In September 2001, Kenyan intelligence officials reported pro-bin Laden graffiti and the unofficial renaming of a Mombasa street as bin Laden Street. These indicate some support for bin Laden and Al Qaeda in Mombasa. Such pockets of sympathizers, people willing to provide cover for terrorists, suggest that the coast region is becoming an incubator for radical Islamic militants — terrorists.

Mombasa was also a key target because of its large number of foreign tourists. The use of nearby airfields by British and German military aircraft, the regular presence of U.S. naval vessels in the port, and the large Muslim population of the coastal region may be other factors. It is sad to think that the Middle East conflict between Israel and Arabs is shifting to Africa and killing innocent Africans. In addition to killing people, terrorism is killing the tourism industry as well.

Tourism or Terrorism?

Recent terrorism could not have come at a worse time for Kenya. Before the Mombasa attacks, pickpockets and annoying hawkers were the main security concerns along Kenya's beaches. A tourist police unit was created. Similarly, in Nairobi, where more serious crime thrives, police kiosks were set up on downtown streets. Now, the seemingly never-ending challenge of making visitors feel secure is only magnified.

Kenya's tour operators point out that the latest attacks were specifically aimed at Israelis and not tourists in general. Tour operators, lodge owners, and others are also playing up the remoteness of their destinations. They say it would take terrorists many hours on rough roads to reach premier lodges in such places as Amboseli National Park, at the foot of Mount Kilimanjaro, or Maasai Mara. Obviously it will take more than assurances to bring them back. Until then, Kenya's economy is going to have a rough ride.

LIFE IN KENYA TODAY

What is life like in Kenya? Today, many people worry about their basic well being. They are deeply concerned about employment and economic survival. And they are becoming increasingly impatient over the ever-present bribery and corruption, and spiraling crime rates. Let us begin with the crime. A recent report by the United Nations Center for Human Settlements indicates that Nairobi is one of the world's most dangerous cities. More than one- third of the 8,600 Nairobi residents participating in the study had been robbed or mugged within the last year. Half of them said they frequently hear gunfire on the streets. Two-thirds of them said they do not feel safe walking in the town even during daylight hours. And a frightening three-fourths of them reported feeling threatened in their own homes after dark. Indeed, a large number of residential burglaries in Nairobi occurred while the owners were at home.

Health care also is a major problem. When Mwai Kibaki was injured in a car accident during the campaign, he did not seek treatment at his local hospital. He went to the airport and boarded a flight to London. Kibaki's injuries were relatively straightforward; he had a broken arm and a sprained ankle. But Kenyan hospitals are unable to provide the level of medical care he wanted. His decision to go abroad was quite typical. In fact, Kenyans and foreigners who can afford to do so frequently travel to developed countries for health care. At the Kenyatta

A woman and her children in their home in Kawangare, a slum of Nairobi. The capital city, once the pride of Africa, has been devastated by government corruption.

National, the nation's best hospital, overcrowding forces two and three patients to share a bed, and technology in the emergency room dates from the late 1970s.

While crime is a very serious problem, most people are more worried about activities of daily living. They are concerned about getting and holding jobs, obtaining adequate food, educating their children, having electricity and water in their homes, and traveling the country's horrible roads. Life for many Kenyans is very tough. Most people blame all their problems on the rampant corruption of the now-gone Moi government. To get a good sense of what is going on, let's visit a middle-class Kenyan home in December 2002.

Meet the Dishkus

James Dishku is a young boy of ten years. He lives near Eldoret in central province with his father, mother, and two younger sisters. He takes school very seriously. Even at such a young age, he realizes that an education is the most important key to success. His father is a struggling farmer and his mother is a seamstress. Neither of them made it past primary school, and it is a major sacrifice to pay his $50 school fees each year. Two of his best friends of the same age, James Karani and Josephine Nyachiro, are not so lucky. Because their parents can't afford the fees, they don't go to school. Under Moi, schooling cost between $12.00 and $192.00 a year per child, depending on family income. James wants to make the best of this opportunity. He hurriedly washes himself with cold, not necessarily clean, water that he hauled from the river earlier this morning. The river is a 15-minute walk away. He pulls on his school uniform, which his mother has just patched up. It is the only one he has, and he must keep it clean. He grabs his bag lunch from the mud floor and runs out the door to meet his friends. They are going to walk together to school, three miles away.

James and his friends arrive at 8:00 A.M., just as school begins. The school is a run-down mud building that is falling apart. A herd of cattle grazes in the field outside the main office. When it rains, all of the children cram into the one room that does not leak in order to keep dry. Classes usually stop until the rain stops. When it is time for classes to start, several of the students are sent home to collect school fees. This is a common occurrence each semester.

The teacher has the only textbook and it is very worn. The public school system is grossly underfunded and can't afford new books. Most of the children in James's class cannot afford to buy their own textbooks. After four hours of learning, they adjourn for lunch and return an hour later for another four hours. At the end of the school day, James and his friends run out of the dingy building, laughing and full of energy, and walk the three miles home.

James's mother, Elizabeth Dishku, began her day around 4:30 A.M. with a crying baby. After making breakfast for her family, she begins working at her sewing job. She is good at sewing and in good times can make about $10.00 to $15.00 a week. There are times, though, when she will go weeks without work. Today is especially promising: a young girl is getting married and needs dresses for herself and her mother. She is expecting them for measuring around 7 A.M., so she has a little time to get herself ready. Her older daughter, Hanna, 7, is old enough to go to school, but they can't afford the school fees. Besides, she knows how to cook and clean fairly well, and is able to take care of the baby while her mother is working.

When her customers arrive, Elizabeth wastes no time. She has posters on the dirt walls showing numerous dress designs and bolts of bold, colorful material. After making their choices and being measured for size, the women get up to leave, promising to be back at the end of the week to pick up their wedding garments. When she asks for some payment, they plead with her to hold off until she has finished. They have no money because they were robbed the day before. At gunpoint, the robbers had taken everything including her engagement ring. When they tried to call the police, they found the phone line was dead as usual. After trudging to the police station, a 30-minute walk away, the police officer asked for *a little something* before he would file their complaint. They left in disgust. Elizabeth sympathizes with them and agrees to receive payment for her services later. "If only life were as easy for us as it is for the wealthy," is Elizabeth's silent lament as she continues her work.

At supper that evening, Elizabeth recounts her customers' robbery experience to a rapt audience. Her husband becomes angry. Crime is so commonplace that nothing is safe anymore and all of the police want *kitu kidogo,* or "a little something." Fred and Mary Nyachiro, Josephine's parents, stop by for a visit. With James and Josephine and the other children playing, the adults begin a serious discussion about life in Kenya.

Fred is unemployed and has unsuccessfully been looking for a job for almost two years. In return for a job offer, everybody wants a little something, which he doesn't have. They have no electricity in their house. His wife is a nurse, but her meager salary is not enough to support their family. That is why Josephine is no longer in school. His extended family can't help either. The husband of his only sister, Mildred Bwire Auma, died of AIDS after infecting her. She married his brother in accordance with local tradition, but he died of AIDS two years later, after infecting two other women. She is sick with the disease and needs help herself. Life is tough, but a future without Moi as president is quite promising.

Alone at last, Elizabeth and her husband, Peter, talk about their own situation. Because of the long drought, the crops have failed. Does it always have to be like this? Without good crops, there will be no money, and without money, James will not make it through school, and without schooling . . . well, his future is bleak. They express their fears and anger about the current situation of Kenya, their beloved country. They fall asleep with heavy hearts, not knowing what the next day will bring.

A new president for a new era! President Mwai Kibaki's victory in the 2002 election helped Kenyans anticipate a happier life for themselves and for their children.

The Future of Kenya – Change

W hen Mr. Kibaki won the December 2002 election in a landslide, Kenya exploded with hope. For the huge crowds cheering and dancing in the streets, it was truly a joyful day. For the many Kenyans who survive on $1 a day and live without electricity and running water, anticipation for a bright future is very high. From rural farming villages to the bars of Nairobi, Kenyans say the end of Moi's rule was the most important turning point in the nation's history. But, what does the future hold for Kenya?

THE GOVERNMENT

President Kibaki's government inherited a badly damaged economy. No quick fixes exist for the poverty, neglect, and decaying infrastructure that resulted from decades of mismanagement.

Unfortunately, quick fixes are exactly what Kenyans are looking for. Without them, the elation and optimism of today may quickly turn to frustration for many people. Even a slight improvement could unlock huge potential.

However, the government faces major problems. A big question is whether NARC, the ruling political party hastily assembled primarily to fight Moi, can stick together long enough to bring real change to Kenya. Formed largely from former KANU politicians and potentially hostile factions united by their common hatred of Moi, the coalition could easily unravel.

Kibaki's anticorruption plans could lead to tension. Many of those who benefited from the old system, some of whom are members of NARC, surely will resist change. There will be strong pressures from within NARC to leave the past alone. Will NARC survive?

THE ECONOMY

Kenya's immediate economic future is in serious jeopardy. A general decline in the global economy is having a drastic impact on the country. Tourism is suffering under the threat of terrorism. The staggering effects of recent droughts will likely linger for some time, even if rains return to normal. But the rainfall patterns continue to be erratic and unpredictable, leading some scientists to suggest that Kenya will suffer from global warming.

The IMF and World Bank are reviewing the Kibaki government's efforts to eliminate corruption. Depending on the outcome, financial aid could begin flowing once again into Kenya. The resumption of aid would bring some temporary relief to Kenyans. However, the usual conditions attached to structural adjustment loans—reduction of government expenditure, removal of government subsidies, and privatization of government enterprises—may create the same problems in Kenya that they have been known to create in other parts of Africa. In short, it will probably get worse before it gets better.

The most promising change will probably be in the realm of infrastructure repair. Assuming the Kibaki government can significantly reduce corruption, international financial aid may be easily secured for rebuilding the deteriorated infrastructure. Improving the roads and railways will restore the free circulation of goods and services and improve the overall economy. For the many Kenyans stuck in poverty, this cannot come quickly enough.

Eliminating Bribery and Corruption

Many Kenyans hope they will no longer have to pay bribes now that Moi is gone. During the inauguration of President Kibaki, crowds took to Moi Avenue outside of city hall and sang to police officers in Swahili, "No More 'Kitu Kidogo,'" or "No More 'a little something.'"

Kenya is going through change, but are the beneficiaries of the old corrupt system ready for change? A week after the new government came to power, the newspapers told the story of one police officer who didn't realize things had changed. He waved down the overloaded matatu as he always did. The driver got out, and duly paid the bribe, as he always did. But the matatu passengers rebelled. They grabbed the money back, as well as all the other crumpled notes gathered that morning, from the hands of astonished police officers. As one passenger said, "President Kibaki pledged to fight corruption. The war starts with us, the citizens."

Kenyans suddenly feel empowered. The question is how long will this feeling last? The problems are so deep. Corruption is so widespread and entrenched that it will take drastic action and perhaps a long time to eliminate. But Kenyans want change—and they want it quickly.

Threat of Terrorism

Unfortunately, terrorism in Kenya is likely to continue. Increasing Islamic militancy worldwide, the concentration of Muslims in the coast province, and the never-ending potential of war in the Middle East make this a strong possibility. Kenyans so far have not been the direct targets of terrorism attacks, but they have been victims. Most likely, they will continue to be victims, as will the nation's tourism industry and its economy in general.

EDUCATION

Barely two weeks after coming into power, the government of Mwai Kibaki abolished the fees primary school students were required to pay to attend class. This fulfilled one of his campaign promises. Classrooms rapidly overflowed with students, however, with the influx of youngsters whose parents had been unable to pay the fees to send their children to class. At one school, angry parents threatened to set the principal's office on fire after school officials announced that classes were full and no more children would be enrolled. One parent in frustration said: "The government declaration that primary education is free and compulsory does not help us when it has not made preparations for its implementation."

This statement appears to characterize all of the challenges facing the Kibaki government. They want to do what is good and right for Kenya, but lack the needed resources. In the Moi years, parents were charged fees and public school enrollment stood at about 85% in Moi's final year, down from 95% in 1990. The government hopes to find the estimated $65 million needed for free primary education, after identifying and stopping the corruption that previously consumed these financial resources.

Corruption involving government ministers and senior officials has historically been rampant in Kenya. Frequently, such corruption is never fully exposed or prosecuted because the justice system is also corrupt. Perhaps, the most notorious case is the Goldenberg scam, in which the Goldenberg Company received $600 million from the government as compensation for exports of gold and diamonds in 1991–1992. Yet, Kenya has no

President Kibaki eliminated fees for primary school students to better educate "the future of Kenya." Hopefully, there will soon be enough teachers, supplies, and facilities for all of the students.

gold or diamond mines; it does not export gold or diamonds. A trial into the scandal began in 1994 but has been repeatedly postponed for unknown reasons (because of corruption?). Recovering only 10% of this money will provide enough for free primary education. The influx of new students is but one sign of change today. Can the money be found to support the schools and sustain this progress?

HIV AND AIDS AND THE HEALTH CARE SYSTEM

HIV-AIDS continues to be a serious problem. At the end of 2001, an estimated 2.5 million Kenyans were living with HIV, the virus that causes AIDS. Of the population aged between 15 and 49, an estimated 15% were infected with the virus. By December 2001, 890,000 children had lost at least one parent to the dreadful disease. In fact, 190,000 people in Kenya died of AIDS during 2001 alone. Unfortunately, deeply entrenched cultural practices may help the spread of HIV to continue. About 700 Kenyans die of AIDS-related illness each day, and AIDS patients occupy about 50% of the country's hospital beds. The provision of drugs that help AIDS patients live longer will be very helpful. Many people question whether the Kibaki government will be able to provide such expensive drugs free or at low cost to Kenya's poor?

Kenya's health care system is in shambles. Underpaid doctors and nurses are leaving their posts and there is a critical shortage of essential medical supplies. Help, however, may be on the way. Charity Kaluki Ngilu, the woman who dared to run for president, is the new Health Minister. One of her first official actions was to fire the head of the Kenyatta Hospital, the country's largest medical center. She promises more changes. Hopefully, soon patients will no longer have to share beds. Again, the primary problem is adequate funding and where it can be obtained. Only time can provide an answer to this difficult question.

CONCLUSION

Before leaving Kenya, let's reflect back on our journey through this beautiful country. Kenya's spectacular physical geography is beyond compare. Few countries can boast of having lush tropical forests and snow—both right on the equator. Kenya is the land of game parks, vast wildlife populations, and safaris. However, population pressure, environmental degradation, and poaching are reducing the stock of wildlife. Terrorism is also eroding tourism, recent terrorists attacks in Nairobi and Mombasa are keeping many tourists away.

The future of this country remains quite unclear and depends largely on the actions of the new government. Ethnic violence may disappear, or it could become worse. If NARC, the current governing political party, holds together, political, ethnic, and national unity should be fostered. If it falls apart along ethnic lines, ethnic conflict surely will escalate. Corruption could get better or worse. This outcome will depend largely on the Kibaki government's efforts. The economy could sputter to life immediately, following resumption of aid money from IMF, World Bank, and other institutions. But long-term improvements will take time, perhaps much longer than most Kenyans would like.

The future for Kenya is quite unpredictable. Only one thing remains certain and that is change. Kenya's corruption-weary people are ready for change and pray that it is positive. Can we join the Dishkus as they pray for good change? That way, we can come back and visit this country and see its wonderful sights and people again. Will you miss the matatus? Finally, with Moi gone, what are Kenyans going to talk about— perhaps the weather?

Facts at a Glance

Country name Republic of Kenya
Conventional- Kenya
Former- British East Africa

Location Eastern Africa, bordering the Indian Ocean, between Somalia and Tanzania

Area total: 224,966 square miles (582,650 square kilometers)

Capital Nairobi

Climate varies from tropical along coast to arid in interior

Terrain low plains rise to central highlands bisected by Great Rift Valley; fertile plateau in west

Elevation lowest point: Indian Ocean 0 ft (0 meters);
highest point: Mount Kenya 17,057 feet (5,199 meters)

Natural Hazards recurring drought; flooding during rainy seasons

Land Use arable land: 7%; permanent crops: 1%; other: 92% (1998 est.)

Environmental Issues water pollution from urban and industrial wastes; degradation of water quality from increased use of pesticides and fertilizers; water hyacinth infestation in Lake Victoria; deforestation; soil erosion; desertification; poaching

Population 31,138,735 (July 2002 est.)

Population Growth Rate 1.15% (2002 est.)

Life Expectancy total population: 47.02 years;
female: 47.85 years (2002 est.);
male: 46.2 years

Nationality Kenyan(s)

Ethnic Groups Kikuyu 22%, Luhya 14%, Luo 13%, Kalenjin 12%, Kamba 11%, Kisii 6%, Meru 6%, other African 15%, non-African (Asian, European, and Arab) 1%

Religions Protestant 45%, Roman Catholic 33%, indigenous beliefs 10%, Muslim 10%, other 2%; Note: a large majority of Kenyans are Christian, but estimates for the percentage of the population that adheres to Islam or indigenous beliefs vary widely.

Languages	English (official), Kiswahili (official), numerous indigenous languages
Literacy	78.1%
Type of Government	Republic
Head of state	President
Independence	December 12, 1963 (from UK)
Administrative divisions	7 provinces and 1 area*; central, coast, eastern, Nairobi area*, north eastern, nyanza, rift valley, western
Flag Description	three equal horizontal bands of black (top), red, and green; the red band is edged in white; a large warrior's shield covering crossed spears is superimposed at the center
Currency	Kenyan shilling (KES)
Gross Domestic Product	$31 billion (2001 est.)
Labor force by occupation	agriculture 75%-80%
Industries	small-scale consumer goods (plastic, furniture, batteries, textiles, soap, cigarettes, flour); agricultural products processing; oil refining, cement; tourism
Exports	$1.8 billion (f.o.b., 2001 est.), tea, horticultural products, coffee, petroleum products, fish, cement
Imports	$3.1 billion (f.o.b., 2001 est.), machinery and transportation equipment, petroleum products, motor vehicles, iron and steel, resins and plastics
Transportation	Railways: total: 1,726 miles (2,778 kilometers) Highways: total: 39,643 miles (63,800 kilometers) Airports: 231 (2001)

1895	British East African Protectorate formed.
Early 1900s	White settlers moved into highlands, railway built from Mombasa to Lake Victoria.
1920	East African Protectorate became crown colony of Kenya—administered by a British governor.

Mau Mau

1944	Kenyan African Union (KAU) formed to campaign for African independence. First African appointment to legislative council.
1947	Jomo Kenyatta became KAU leader.
1952	Secret Kikuyu guerrilla group known as Mau Mau began violent campaign against white settlers. State of emergency declared. Kenyatta arrested.
1953	Kenyatta charged with management of Mau Mau and jailed. KAU banned.
1956	Mau Mau rebellion put down after thousands are killed, mainly Africans.
1959	Kenyatta released from jail but under house arrest.
1960	State of emergency ended. Britain announced plans to prepare Kenya for majority African rule. Kenya African National Union (Kanu) formed by Tom Mboya and Oginga Odinga.
1961	Kenyatta freed and assumed presidency of KANU.
1963	Kenya gained independence, with Kenyatta as prime minister.
1964	Republic of Kenya formed. Kenyatta became president and Odinga vice president.
1966	Odinga, a Luo, left KANU after ideological split, formed rival Kenya People's Union (KPU).
1969	Assassination of government minister Tom Mboya sparked ethnic unrest. KPU banned and Odinga arrested. KANU only political party to contest elections.
1974	Kenyatta re-elected.

Moi Era Begins

1978	Kenyatta died in office, succeeded by Vice President Daniel arap Moi.
1982	**June** Kenya officially declared a one-party state by National Assembly.

August   Army suppressed air force coup attempt. Private Hezekiah Ochuka ruled country for about six hours.

1987   Opposition groups suppressed. International criticism rose of political arrests and human rights abuses.

1989   Political prisoners freed.

1990   Death of the Minister of Foreign Affairs and International Co-operation, Dr. Robert Ouko, in suspicious circumstances led to increased dissent against government.

MultiParty Elections

1991   **August**   Forum for the Restoration of Democracy (FORD) formed by six opposition leaders, including Oginga Odinga. Party outlawed and members arrested. Creditors suspend aid to Kenya amid fierce international condemnation.

December   Special conference of KANU agreed to introduce a multiparty political system.

1992   Approximately 2,000 people killed in tribal conflict in the west of the country.

August   FORD split into two factions—FORD-Asili (led by ex-government minister Kenneth Matiba) and FORD-Kenya (led by Odinga).

December   Moi reelected in multiparty elections. KANU won strong majority.

1994   Odinga died. Opposition groups formed coalition—the United National Democratic Alliance—but it is plagued by disagreements.

1995   New opposition party—Safina—launched by palaeontologist Richard Leakey. Party refused official registration until November 1997.

1997   Demonstrations called for democratic reform. World Bank withheld disbursement of $5 billion in structural adjustment credit.

December   Moi won further term in widely criticized elections. Main opponents facing Moi were former vice president Mwai Kibaki and Raila Odinga, son of Oginga Odinga.

1998   **August**   Bomb exploded at U.S. embassy in Nairobi, killing over 230 people and wounding thousands.

1999 Moi appointed Richard Leakey to head government drive against corruption.

2000 Severe drought in northwest Kenya.

2001 **April** Leakey appeared in court to face charges of abuse of power and perverting the course of justice.

June 11 Moi reshuffled cabinet and appointed opposition party leader Raila Odinga as energy minister in the first coalition government in Kenya's history.

October Moi appointed Kenyatta's son, Uhuru Kenyatta, to parliament and to a cabinet post in November, apparently to rejuvenate the KANU party leadership before the 2003 election.

December Circumcision of girls under the age of 17 banned. Ethnic tensions continued, culminating in several violent clashes. Thousands fled and several people were killed in rent battles involving Nubian and Luo communities in Nairobi's Kibera slum district.

2002 **July** A number of opposition parties formed the National Alliance Party of Kenya to battle KANU in forthcoming general elections.

November Ten Kenyans and three Israelis were killed when an Israeli-owned hotel near Mombasa is blown up by a car bomb. A simultaneous rocket attack on an Israeli airliner failed. A statement—purportedly from the Al Qaeda network—claimed responsibility.

December NARC presidential candidate, Mwai Kibaki, won a landslide victory in general elections, ending Daniel arap Moi's 24-year rule and KANU's four decades in power.

A. Fedders, C. Salvadori, *Peoples and Cultures of Kenya*. Nairobi.: Transafrica, 1982.

H. Finlay, M. Fletcher, G. Crowther, *Kenya*. Oakland, CA: Lonely Planet Publications, 2000.

W. Kairi, *Kenya*. Austin, TX: Raintree/Steck, 2000.

Harold D. Nelson, *Kenya. A Country Study*. Washington, D.C.: American University, Area Handbook Series, Library of Congress, 1984.

Robert Paterson, *Kenya: Cultures of the World*. California: Benchmark Books, 1995.

II. Tichy, *The Magical World of Kenya*. Innsbruck, Austria.: Pinguin Verlag, 1980.

Websites

Kenya Embassy
www.kenyaembassy.com

CIA World Fact Book 2002—Kenya.
http://www.cia.gov/cia/publications/factbook/geos/ke.html

Africa Online—General coverage on Kenya
http://www.africaonline.co.ke/AfricaOnline/kenya/chapter1b1.html

British Broadcasting Corporation—Country Profile.
http://news.bbc.co.uk/2/hi/africa/country_profiles/1024563.stm

Game Parks, Wildlife and Safari
http://kenya.geopassage.com/resources/resources.asp?Sec_ID=3&Con_ID=14

Education—Harambee Schools
http://www.hsk.org.uk/intro.htm

Index

Index

Infrastructure. *See* Energy resources; Telephones; Transportation
Initiation, 50-51, 62-63
International Monetary Fund (IMF), 83, 88, 89, 90, 91, 97, 110, 115
Islam, 31, 47, 71, 102, 111-112
Israel
    and terrorist attack on Paradise Hotel, 10, 97, 100-102, 114
    tourists from, 96
Italy, tourists from, 96

Jesus, Fort, 32-33

Kalenjin tribe, 46, 61
Kamba tribe, 39, 46, 72
Karani, James, 105
Karumba, Kung'u, 40
Kenya African National Union (KANU), 13, 41, 81, 82, 84, 86, 87, 110
Kenya Airways, 91
Kenya Colony, 34
Kenya, Mount, 11, 13, 17, 18, 20, 21, 22, 73
Kenyan African Democratic Union (KADU), 41, 81
Kenyan African Union (KAU), 37, 38, 40
Kenya People's Union (KPU), 82
Kenyatta, Jomo, 36, 38, 39, 40, 41-43, 46, 81-82, 85, 87
Kenyatta, Uhuru, 86, 99
Kenyatta Hospital, 103-104, 114
Kericho, 35
Kibaki, Mwai, 13, 46, 86, 87, 91, 98-99, 103, 109-110, 111, 112, 114, 115
Kibe, Mike, 58
Kibera, 48
Kikuyu Central Association (KCA), 36
Kikuyu tribe, 30, 34, 35, 39, 40, 41, 42, 46, 81
Kinship, 49-50, 97-98
Kisii tribe, 46
Kisumu, 34, 68, 76, 91
Kitale, 35

Lakes, 11, 17, 18, 21, 22, 23-26, 30, 34, 75, 76, 91, 94

Land distribution, 23, 34, 35-36, 41, 81, 88
Languages, 13, 30, 31, 46, 77
Leakey family, 29
Life expectancy, 66
Lingua franca, 46-47
Livestock, 11, 23, 45, 61, 70, 72, 105
Lobelias, 22
Location, 11, 18, 20, 31
Luo tribe, 30, 41, 42, 46, 53, 55, 56, 81, 82
Luya tribe, 46

Maasai Mara Game Reserve, 95
Maasai tribe, 30, 34, 35, 49, 51, 56, 61-63, 72
Maize (corn), 58-60, 74
Makanga (tout), 78, 79
Malindi, 32
Mangrove forests, 22
Mara River, 21-22
Market towns, 76
Marriage, 50, 51-55, 63
Masters and Servants Ordinance of 1906, 36
Matatus (minibuses), 77-79, 91, 111
Mau Mau conflict, 37-41
Mazrui dynasty, 33
Mboya, Tom, 41, 42, 82
Meru tribe, 30, 46, 72
Mining, 11, 90, 112-113
Moi, Daniel arap, 13, 14, 46, 47-48, 82-84, 85-86, 87, 96-97, 98, 105, 107, 111, 112
Moi Day, 85-86
Mombasa, 9-10, 14, 31, 32-33, 34, 56, 60, 71-72, 91, 96-97, 114
    terrorist attack against Paradise Hotel in, 10, 97, 100-102, 114
Mombasa-Uganda railway, 34, 35, 71
Monsoon winds, 31
Motto. *See Harambee*
Mountains, 9, 11, 13, 17, 18, 20, 21, 22, 75, 93
Music, 49, 76, 96
Muslims, 70
Mzungu (whites), 35, 36, 38

Index

page:

8: New Millennium Images
12: © 2003 maps.com
16: New Millennium Images
19: © 2003 maps.com
25: New Millennium Images
26: New Millennium Images
28: John Leicester/AP/Wide World Photos
33: © Jan Butchofsky-Houser/Corbis
37: Hulton Getty Photo Archive/NMI
42: Hulton Getty Photo Archive/NMI
44: New Millennium Images
50: New Millennium Images
54: AFP/NMI
59: New Millennium Images

62: New Millennium Images
64: New Millennium Images
73: New Millennium Images
74: New Millennium Images
78: KRT/NMI
80: AFP/NMI
85: Reuters Photo Archive/NMI
89: Reuters Photo Archive/NMI
92: New Millennium Images
99: KRT/NMI
100: Reuters Photo Archive/NMI
104: KRT/NMI
108: AFP/NMI
113: New Millennium Images

Cover: © Torleif Svensson/CORBIS

About the Author

JOSEPH R. OPPONG is Associate Professor of Geography at the University of North Texas in Denton, Texas, and a native of Ghana. He has about 15 years university teaching experience in Ghana, Canada, and the United States. Joseph has served as Chair of the Africa Specialty Group of the Association of American Geographers and as Director of the Medical Geography Specialty Group. His research focuses on medical geography: the geography of disease and health care. Joseph enjoys teaching, research, photography, and his four children, including Esther, the oldest and co-author of this book.

ESTHER D. OPPONG is an active junior in high school. Her hobbies include talking to and meeting people, writing, singing, and playing her guitar. This is her second book and she dreams of writing many more.

CHARLES F. ("FRITZ") GRITZNER is Distinguished Professor of Geography at South Dakota University in Brookings. He is now in his fifth decade of college teaching and research. During his career, he has taught more than 60 different courses, spanning the fields of physical, cultural, and regional geography. In addition to his teaching, he enjoys writing, working with teachers, and sharing his love for geography with students. As consulting editor for the MODERN WORLD NATIONS series, he has a wonderful opportunity to combine each of these "hobbies." Fritz has served as both president and executive director of the National Council for Geographic Education and has received the Council's highest honor, the George J. Miller Award for Distinguished Service.